365

We

for Women

365 Words of Well-Being for Women

Rachel Snyder

CB

CONTEMPORARY BOOKS

Library of Congress Cataloging-in-Publication Data

Snyder, Rachel.

    365 words of well-being for women / Rachel Snyder.

       p. cm.

    ISBN 0-8092-3079-8

    1. Women—Psychology—Miscellanea. 2. Self-actualization
(Psychology)—Miscellanea. I. Title.

    HQ1206.S662 1997

    158′.1′082—dc20   96-36776

                                       CIP

Cover design by Kim Bartko
Cover illustration copyright © Jennie Oppenheimer/Stock Illustration Source
Author photograph by Judith Phillips Photography
Interior design by Nancy Freeborn

Kelly,

This book is dedicated to you,
and to the infinite spirit of well-being
that lies within you.

Enjoy these "words"

Much love,
A.S.

July 11/97.

Acknowledgments

In Autumn 1994, the seed for this book was planted in the fertile Berkshire Hills of western Massachusetts, in the office of *The Women's Times*. Publisher Eugenie Sills and then-editor Maria Black asked me for a quick feature on things women could do to stay well. "Maybe a list of some kind," they offered. "Just write about what you and your friends do to be well," they added. Four days later, "The Seven Words of Well-Being for Women" were born: *Move, Touch, Listen, Feel, Trust, Gather, Receive.* The piece took me forty-one years and forty-five minutes to write. Much love and thanks, Eugenie, for providing a place where I could create, support, laugh, play, write, blossom, belong, and appreciate more than ever the awesome power of women's words.

I am deeply grateful for whatever angel sent me Barbara Ciletti, my self-proclaimed mentor as well

Introduction

You may think this is a book about words, but it's really a book about freedom. The freedom to be the woman you were always destined to be, and to be her with a powerful sense of well-being.

This is a book about remembering—to live, love, trust, cry, surrender, dance, and sing. To take the time to discover who you really are, to feel more deeply, to ask for help when you need it, and to receive that help with gratitude. It is a simple book, filled with simple things you can do to grow and create and move and reweave the life that you yearn for and richly deserve.

You'll find yourself in these pages. Maybe not on every page, but somewhere, you'll find yourself. You'll find your friends, your mother, your sister, your daughter. You'll see yourselves giggling, howling, protecting, nurturing, forgiving, rebelling, and collapsing on the floor. You'll be standing up to fight and sitting down to rest. Once in a while, you'll even kvetch a little. You'll be cooking and eating, praising your personal version of Spirit, transforming yourselves and your world.

These 365 words give you a recipe for living more fully the life that only you can live. With a bit of this and a bit of that and a pinch of the other, you can concoct a glorious stew that is often sweet and sometimes bitter. Now and then, you'll dine alone in the darkness, and that's okay, too.

You don't have to live all these words all the time. In fact, if you don't want to, you don't have to live any of them (see *Defy*). Yet I invite you to consider each one carefully, and to know that women like you and women not at all like you have found great joy and strength when they have embraced these words and the actions they inspire.

Use this book as you will. Choose a word for each day of the year or for each day of the week. Choose it with your eyes open or eyes closed. Let the book fall open and let the words be chosen for you. Reflect on the words and think about what they mean to you. Speak the words out loud. Whisper them or shout them. Sing them or chant them, paint them, string them into necklaces, write them on your hand, wallpaper your dining room with them, or copy them and stick them on your refrigerator. Take your words to other women and toss them around the circle. Rewrite these words, add some new ones, or pick your own words altogether.

It takes a lifetime to live these words and all they represent. A lifetime of self-discovery and self-creation. A lifetime of struggle, of wondering where you belong, of testing and tasting and letting go and bringing forth your own glorious self. It may often feel as though you're going nowhere, but trust that you are always exactly where you need to be.

I have lived many of these words, yet there are others I still have yet to claim. I offer them now when you can use them most to be joyous, be whole, and be well.

Rachel Snyder
Boulder, Colorado

365 Words of Well-Being for Women

Accept

Recognize what you can change and what you can't. In every moment, accept that everything is as it should be. Accept that your body is round and fat and glorious. Just love it. Accept that you don't do things the way everyone else does. Just embrace it. Accept that sometimes your belly hurts, sometimes you don't have enough money to pay the light bill, sometimes life is too hard. Just cry and move through it. Accept that you can't do it all—and who would want to, anyway? Accept a kind word. Don't apologize. Accept a gift—no matter how big, how small. Say *Thank you* without embarrassment. Accept that life isn't always fair and find the wonder in that, too. Don't accept things that aren't yours, like misdirected shame and blame. Like credit for someone else's accomplishment. Like disrespect. Accept everything you are and nothing you are not.

Ache

Feel deep down inside the pain of missing someone or something so badly it hurts. Notice the
empty spaces around your heart that need filling. Tune into other aches in your body. When
your belly burns with a red-hot fire, pay attention. What is the true source of your ache?
What are you trying to digest that's too large,
too hot, too unfamiliar to handle? Ache for the
friend who died of AIDS too early. Ache for the
mothering you never received, the love you had
and then lost, the love you never had at all.
Ache to be held, to be touched, to be adored.
Ache for the sad woman down the block, the
frightened child upstairs, the grieving parents
around the corner. Let your heart ache and
break and ache again—until it grows stronger
and more able to open with ease.

Act

When it's time, get moving.
After you've reflected and meditated, waited, prayed, and reaffirmed, act. Act on your instincts. Act without delay. Send the letter. Make the call. Pack the box. Issue the invitation. Get on the plane. Act already! Act with your own best interests at heart. Act in accordance with your most closely held values. Act mindfully. Act on behalf of the very young or the very old or the very needy. Now and then, act half your age. Act out in your own living room, act up in public. Strut around and act as though you own the joint. Act like the woman you've always wanted to be—and don't act surprised when suddenly you are!

Admire

Admire other women and let them know exactly how you feel. Admire them because they lived in the White House or because they built their own white house with their own two hands. Admire them because they danced and sang their way across Broadway or because they danced an old Irish jig every Sunday at the local nursing home. Admire a woman because she raised two great kids single-handedly; admire a woman who kept a marriage thriving and alive for more than fifty-two years. Admire a plain woman who turns heads with her ever-present smile. Admire the grandmother who took on a new family when her goddaughter died. Admire that woman in the newspaper for her grit and determination. Admire the woman who never got into the newspaper for her selfless devotion to the dying. Tell her *I admire you*. Write a note that says so. While you're at it, remember to drop yourself a postcard, too.

Adorn

Show the world the glorious goddess that lives within you. When everyone else is wearing shapeless T-shirts and running shoes, wear a sundress that ripples in the slightest breeze. If you like fingernail polish, wear it! Ditto for your toes. If you're the only woman on the crew, wear hot pink lipstick and thirteen earrings just to drive home the point. Take a hint from the women of India, from the Rom women of Eastern Europe, from Native American elders and Mexican señoritas. Make every day a celebration by dressing the part. Let your body be a canvas for colorful creations. Add one bracelet this week and three the next. Wear as much makeup as you want. Get a tattoo or three or four. Wear flowers in your hair, ribbons at your throat, silk at your waist, and bells on your toes. If that's not your style, keep your adornments under wraps for select eyes only.

Allow

Allow yourself to ask for what you need. Allow
yourself to need help, to need love, to need
other people. Give yourself permission to say
This is what I need, to say it without shame,
without guilt. Now allow yourself to receive
what is offered. Allow yourself to be human.
Allow yourself the luxury of screwing up now
and then, of being less than perfect. Allow yourself to lay it all down and breathe. Now allow
someone else to help you pick up the pieces.
Give her permission to love you in the only way
she knows how. Every so often, allow yourself to
forget about the bills and the phone calls and
the deadlines. Allow yourself the freedom to feel
exactly how you feel, to be exactly where you are
in any given moment. Allow others the freedom
to do the same.

Appreciate

Appreciate your friends. Appreciate the time she picked you up after your operation, even when it was snowing so hard. Appreciate that she listened when you needed to talk. Needed to be heard. Needed to cry. Appreciate whoever mowed your lawn the day of the funeral. Appreciate whoever found your overdue video, returned it, *and* paid the fine. When friends are in short supply, learn to appreciate being with yourself. Appreciate having a job where you don't have to wear a dress. Appreciate having a job where you do. Appreciate that your body can take you where you want to go. If it can't, appreciate that your mind can take you there instead. Appreciate the good men in your life. Tell them you appreciate them, and appreciate that they're learning to be well just like you.

Ask

Wishing doesn't make it so. Ask, and you at least have a chance. Ask anybody, ask everybody, ask God. Ask for help with the dishes. Ask for a ride because you don't have a car. Ask what it's going to take for you to get a promotion. Ask a friend for a loan of $2,000. Ask a beloved to hold you just one luscious minute more. When a stranger asks how old you are, ask *Why does it matter?* Ask someone over for breakfast, then ask whether they want hot fudge or peanut butter on their ice cream. Ask the Goddess if you can crawl into her lap and lay your head on her big beautiful breasts. Ask yourself why it's so hard to ask. And even harder to receive. When the brownies are absolutely divine, ask for the recipe. When the seminar is terminally boring, ask to be excused.

Attract

Like a high-powered magnet, attract to yourself everything you desire. Attract the right job by being impeccably clear about what you want—and why. (Making some calls and sending a few letters won't hurt either!) Attract the money you need by affirming your worthiness and your willingness to receive. (Taking an action step or two won't hurt either!) To attract loving relationships, be as kind, as caring, as attractive as the people you want to meet. Anticipate the worst—and you're certain to attract it. To attract joy, embrace joy. To attract a spiritual teacher, quit whining and start accepting that you *are* one. To have friends, be one. To gain respect, respect yourself first and then move on to everyone around you. *Everyone!*

Awaken

Wake up! Refuse to sleepwalk through your life any longer. Wake up! Open your eyes and dare to see the world in a new and different way. Wake up! Awaken your passion for life and awaken it in those around you. Awaken yourself spiritually. Find something larger than yourself to believe in. Find a way to lift yourself above the mundane. Wake up! Smell the coffee! Take a long, hard look at all you've been missing, and decide not to miss any more. Awaken your senses, your intuition, your desires. Awaken the parts of yourself that have been sleeping: the lover, the trickster, the artist, the maiden, the crone. Wake up, and don't go back to sleep. Life is a dream, and to live it, you must be awake.

Bake

Bake bread the old-fashioned way. Bake muffins crammed full of blueberries. Bake exotic cakes with unpronounceable names and multicolored frostings. Bake tortillas, flatbreads, scones, cookies, biscotti. Make little people out of dough and bake them into life. Make them elves, hobbits, gremlins with vests and boots and long beards and braids, and hang them on trees or walls or shelves. Bake because it smells like the very best kitchen you ever remember, because it feels good to have flour on your hands and vanilla on your fingers. Bake because you want to lick the whole bowl yourself without asking anyone's permission. Bake because you really enjoy wearing an apron. Bake because women have always baked and always will, and only by baking will you understand why.

Balance

When you find yourself teetering too far in one direction, bring some balance back into your life. Balance your work time with playtime. Balance your social butterflying with quiet, uninterrupted periods of solitude. If you've been giving too much, let everyone know you're ready to receive. Balance your diet. Too much of any one thing— no matter how good—can never be good. If you've been running around at breakneck speed, slow down before an accident or injury does it for you. If you've been sitting in front of a screen (any screen!) for too long, get up from your chair and dance or walk or swim or stretch. When you feel like you've been balancing too many things for too long, put some down. Do it slowly and mindfully, so you don't lose your balance while you do.

Bargain

Don't ever consider paying retail. Offer five to start, and expect to pay three by the time you're done. All right, settle for four. Prowl through consignment shops and thrift shops and upscale second-hand shops. Ask for a 25 percent discount because the button is falling off. All right, settle for 15 percent. Offer ninety-nine cents for that last piece of pie, the one with the broken crust and the forlorn filling. When your boss offers you a raise, bargain for fewer hours instead. When your partner offers to watch the kids for an afternoon, bargain until you've got yourself a three-day weekend. Use your bargaining power to empower yourself. Come to the bargaining table with your eyes wide open—just in case you're hit with a lot more than you bargained for.

Bask

Bask in the warmth of the summer sun. When your friend finishes college after twenty years, bask in the glow of her joy. Take off all your clothes and bask in the moonlight. When your mother finally becomes a U.S. citizen, bask in the light of her smile. Bask in another woman's glory without needing to snatch any of it for yourself. Bask in the presence of a newborn child no matter whose it is. Walk into a well-tended garden and bask in the colors and the scents and the profusion of textures. Just drink it in. Let the crisp autumn air wash over you; let the serenity of a windswept grassy plain envelop you. When you walk into a room overflowing with a sacred hush, bask in it. When everyone in your family is in one room, bask in it. Don't talk, don't question, don't ask, just bask.

Bathe

Make your bathtub your temple. Purify and anoint yourself to begin the day or end the day or for no particular reason at all. Drizzle coconut oil or lavender oil onto your skin and watch it shine in the glow of a candle. Listen to music or make your own. Read something, write something. Wash away the annoyances and aggravations that have been clinging to your skin all day. Imagine every drop of water finding its way to those brittle, cracked, dried-up places in your soul. Scoop up water in your hands or in a cloth or in a cup and let it drip over your face, your belly, your breasts. Prepare yourself for your own sacred, secret ritual. Stay in as long as you like, and emerge guilt-free and dry. Tell yourself how beautiful you are and believe every glistening word of it.

Be

Remember that life is in the being, not the doing. Be every bit of everything that you are. Be tough, be soft, be dramatic, be subdued. Be a little bit of this and a little bit of that. Be the one who always shows up on time or be the one who lives according to her own inner clock. Be the one who never forgets a detail or be the one who never remembers. Be happy when you feel like it and be sad when you're down. Be who you are—not who they told you you should be. Be able to cry in front of someone you hardly know, if it's time to cry. Be willing to be real. Be talkative if you are; be quiet if you're not. Be ready to drop your masks and your protective armor and be genuine. Be in the moment, be in the light.

And just when they think they know exactly who you are, be prepared to be something altogether different.

Befriend

Make a new friend. Walk up to the woman in the park and say *You look like a woman I would like to be friends with*. Strike up a conversation and go where it leads you. Befriend someone who looks not at all like you. Someone whose skin is different, whose hair is different, whose shoes and clothes are utterly different. Befriend someone thirty years older than you or thirty years younger. Befriend the person in line who's buying something you would never purchase in a million years. Befriend the woman who sips coffee while tears stream down her face. Befriend a child, befriend a friendly dog. Befriend a street person, a person who asks you for money, a person who seems more lost than you can ever imagine being, and then look past all of that and be a real friend.

Begin

Start something. Put one foot in front of the other and inch forward ever so slightly. Show up. Say *Hello* and begin a conversation. Ask *Says who?* and begin a revolution. Write one sentence and begin your novel. Begin again, this time in a different key, at a different tempo. Begin putting yourself first. Begin enjoying it. Begin an intentional community if that's how you want to live. Begin a reading group and focus on women who made bold new beginnings. Begin a new way of eating, a new way of moving, a new way of getting your needs met. Begin as soon as you finish reading this page. Begin at the beginning and don't even think about where it will take you. Now begin.

Believe

Believe in the power of believing. Say *I believe* and believe it. Believe in fairy tales for what they can teach you about real life. Believe in happy endings, and believe that they don't always happen. Believe in something, *anything*, that gives you the courage and strength to continue on when it would be so easy to give up. Believe it when a friend says you're beautiful. Believe it when you hear the words *You deserve to be happy*. When someone tells you something, believe the parts that feel right, that resonate in your belly, and discard the rest. Believe that you have choices and that you can choose wisely. Believe your own instincts above anyone else's. Believe that you can do more with your life than you're doing, and then do it. Above all, believe in yourself. When something seems truly unbelievable, it may be worth believing.

Can you believe that?

Belong

Find something you can belong to. A pack of wolves just like you. A coven. A circle of women who get together to quilt and talk. A professional networking group. A softball team. A choir that sings Bulgarian chants. Belong to a group of people who share something—a love of Beethoven, a keen fascination with bats. A deep connection to Renaissance Europe. Find a group you can call your own. Or create one. Know you can turn to these people when you need a favor. Need a lift. Need a shoulder. Every woman belongs somewhere, with some other women. Find your group by asking around. By advertising. By putting a flyer on a bulletin board. Keep looking and know they're looking for you. Once you begin in earnest, it won't be long until you belong.

Bliss

Bliss out.

Bliss out on joy, bliss out on pleasure, bliss out on love. When you think you've reached the ceiling of your bliss, ride the bliss train right on through. Bliss out on nature. Bliss out on the smell of pine, the feel of moss on your cheek, the awesome, sweet tartness of wild mountain cherries. Sit in a circle and drum and rattle and dance your way into bliss. Bliss out in the presence of anything newborn. Bliss out beneath a golden sun in a cloudless sky, beneath a shimmering full moon, below a never-ending canopy of starlight. Sit at the fire's edge and bliss out. Bliss out on watermelon and on handmade tortillas and fresh-from-the-garden salsa and on strawberries dipped in chocolate. Call up the Bliss Goddess, and when she walks in, bliss on out.

Blossom

When it's time, when you can't wait another moment, unfold your petals and display your grandeur. Do it when you're twenty-eight or when you're fifty-three or when you're eighty-four. Open up to the world with a glow and an attitude that says *Yes, now I am really here.* Pick up a paintbrush, a hammer, a baseball. Go to law school, learn to drive, take swimming lessons, run for office. Send out announcements. Throw yourself a party. Because now your time has come and the world had better make room for you like never before. Just like a magnificent flower, you'll go from tightly closed and protected to full and fragrant and open and unforgettable. Whether you're an early bloomer or a late bloomer, one thing is sure: you will feel as though you've waited forever, only to burst forth "overnight" when you least expect it.

Braid

Braid a young girl's thick and curly hair, an old woman's thin and graying hair. Dreadlocks and cornrows and skinny little braids that remind you that your hair is growing. Glorious braids of a different sort on the head of a woman who has lost her hair. Sit together on the front step and braid your sister's hair in the sun. Sit bareback on a horse and braid its mane. Sinew, yarn, cloves of garlic, flower garlands, weeds, beads, long and shimmering strands of purple, turquoise, aqua, crimson satin ribbons—braid them and hang them from doorways and off the brims of straw hats and in your car and from the handlebars of your bicycle. Braid big, eggy loaves of challah and sprinkle them with seeds. Look long and hard at braids, how they join many single strands into one sturdy, elegant, and simple whole. Gently intertwine your body, mind, and spirit, and remember not to pull too tight.

Break

Make a clean break. Break the news gently. Break free of limitations, and stop believing they can ever break you. If your gut tells you that this marriage will never work, break it off before you're in too deep. If anyone ever gave you a break, pass it on to a woman who needs a break right now. Reconsider making any vow you'll want to break later. If you're part of a cycle of violence and abuse, break it. Break the silence and shame. Break the old patterns that held back your grandmother, your mother, your sisters—and that threaten to hold you back, too.

Remember that a breakthrough often feels like a breakdown—and that when your heart fully opens, it may feel like it first has to break.

Breakfast

Breakfast alone when the morning's still new.
Breakfast light, breakfast quiet. Breakfast big,
with pancakes and French toast and eggs and
muffins and croissants and big bowls of fruit
and little bowls of marmalade and preserves.
Breakfast on a boat, before the fish are biting.
Breakfast with a friend. Breakfast at a diner at
three-thirty in the afternoon. Breakfast reading
the obituaries, reading the comics, reading the
stock finals. Breakfast writing notes to friends
who can read them while they breakfast. Breakfast in camp, sitting on the ground. Breakfast in
a hotel, with a white linen napkin laid fresh in
your lap. Breakfast with clients, breakfast with
champions. If you miss breakfast, be thankful
there's lunch.

Breathe

In-spire yourself. For just a moment—or twelve moments— notice the rhythm of your own breathing in and breathing out. Watch your belly swell, then feel the breath move up your body until it swirls around your heart with a warm, reddish glow and finally leaves your lips with a sigh. Breathe fast, breathe hard, until you tingle from the tips of your toes to the crown of your head and you can actually feel the feel of being alive. When you feel yourself clutching, breathe. When you most want to catch your breath, let it go. Breathe along with another person, looking into another pair of eyes. Don't stop breathing. Don't stop the breath. Breathe.

Bring

Bring your gifts to the circle. Bring your
heart, your song, your prayer. Bring
your willingness to be open, to listen, to
hold another human in your arms.
Bring what you alone can bring. Bring
your strong hands, your singular understanding of old truck engines, your
freshly oiled chain saw. Bring your laptop, your love of quantum physics, your
ancient Chinese wisdom. When asked to
bring something, bring a bottle or two
of home brew, of tarragon vinegar, of
homemade amazake. Bring your drum,
your favorite poem, the comic strip that
cracked you up. Bring the letter from
your dear friend in Bosnia, the one
where she talks about having to scour
the streets for bread, and when the talk
turns to TV sitcom characters, bring the
letter out of your pocket and bring
everyone back to reality.

Brush

Brush your hair one hundred strokes every day.
Now someone else's. Now brush your dog,
your cat, your horse, singing softly all the
while. Brush a feather against your own cheek.
Now someone else's. Watch them shiver. Brush
away a tear with the side of your index finger
and then lick the salt from your own body.
Brush up against someone and notice the
energy change form. Brush bread crumbs off
the counter into your waiting palm. Use a corn
broom to brush every ash off the hearth in
time for summer. Brush the spider gently back
onto the floor. Shine up every corner of your
room with a scrub brush, with a tiny broom.
Brush up on all the languages you know, even
your own. Sit on the bow of a sailboat and
brush your hair out of your eyes; sit on the
edge of the bathtub and brush your teeth.

Build

Pick up a hammer and build something. Anything. Build a tower of blocks or socks or stones, castles in the sand, or tiny villages made of clay. Build up your body in places that are weak, build up your friendships in places that are strong. Lay down foundations that can withstand building, tearing down, and rebuilding. Build a lodge out back, a moon hut just for women, a tipi. Build it with your bare hands, with saplings that have fallen in the forest, with lumber you mill with a friend. Build that fireplace you saw in a glossy magazine. When it's done, build a fine fire in it. In your mind's eye, watch the flames burn down all the walls you've built between yourself and others.

Out of the ashes, build something new.

Burn

Burn leaves in autumn. Burn sage and sweetgrass to purify your room and yourself. Burn the
old pictures, the old letters, the old papers that
no longer mean anything. Burn candles everywhere, inside and out, in glass holders and old
pie tins and in seashells on window sills and
counters and tabletops. Cast into the fire those
feelings and attitudes that no longer serve you.
Feel them disintegrate. Watch how the smoke
curls. Burn off anger in small doses. Don't wait
for a meltdown. Create the hearth that contains
and focuses your inner fire. Burn the dinner and
then laugh about it. If it's necessary for your
self-survival, yes, burn a bridge every now and
then. Just make sure you're safely on one side or
the other before you do.

Care

Care for yourself as much as you care for others. If you care enough to do something about another's pain and suffering, care enough to do something about your own. Care whether she's had a rotten day, and care enough to tell her so. Care enough to speak up when someone fouls your planet. Care about the old, the young, the sick, and insist that your elected officials care, too. Care lovingly for your belongings so they will last longer. Care lovingly for your friendships so they will last a lifetime. Care whether you get the worst table in a restaurant. Care whether your new jacket rips a week after you bought it. Make sure the store cares, too. Care whether there are still wild, sacred places you can visit in silence. Care whether the movie includes thirty-four murders and seven rapes, and demand that Hollywood care, too. Care that babies are having babies and that babies are killing babies. Whenever you want to say *I don't care*, ask yourself *If not me, then who?*

Caress

Caress your shoulder while you're thinking. Caress another's shoulder while you're not. Caress a piece of antique linen or silk or lace. Caress a piece of handmade paper. Let your fingers glide over the ridges and veins. Caress a quartz crystal and feel its energy. Run your fingertips up and down a peacock feather, around the contours of a chunk of alabaster, over a fuzz-faced peach. Never pass up the chance to caress a baby's bottom. Or ear. Or toe. When there's no baby around, do the same to someone older. Or to yourself. Roll a silken lotion scented with coconut or sandalwood or roses between your thumb and forefinger—or between *all* your fingers. Then yes oh yes oh yes, caress!

Caretake

Before you can caretake others, take care to take care of yourself. Take care of your arms so you can lift another up. Take care of your own heart so you can inspire another to open hers. Take care of your mind so you remain a clear and focused guide. Only then are you ready to caretake an elder, an infant, an invalid. Caretake the living, the dying, the injured, the fallen. Caretake a school, a house, a farm, that tiny park that no one else seems to care about. Caretake an organization that is floundering, a neighborhood that's crumbling, a woman who has lost her way. Take time to care mindfully and to care well. Most important, take care you don't give up your entire life by taking care of everyone but yourself.

Carol

Sing the songs of the season. Songs of harvest, songs of praise, songs of freedom and light and miracles. Songs of spring-a-coming-in and winter gone away. Carol in groups small or large, sing songs old and new. Sing around a piano, an organ, a CD player, a dulcimer, a lute. Sing by the hearth, sing in the field, sing alongside a quietly babbling brook, sing in the square. Carol while strolling the neighborhood, on a hay wagon, packed inside a horse-drawn sleigh, in an open car. Sing rounds and ballads and four-part harmonies, and fill the air with mirth and good cheer. Sing arm-in-arm, dance while you carol, step lively, and make a joyful noise for all to hear.

Carry

Carry yourself with queenly grace. Carry the memory of an unforgettable moment. Carry a bag of food to someone who needs it. Carry a child as much as you can, as close as you can, yet stop the moment it begins to hurt or you begin to feel resentful. Carry a sign in a picket line to show you support the women whose jobs are on that line. Carry on a conversation only as long as you want; then end it. Offer to carry a sack for a woman who's carrying her unborn child. Carry a song in your heart. Stop carrying forty-seven suitcases of emotional baggage. Carry things to their natural conclusion. Allow someone else—another woman perhaps—to carry you over an emotional threshold. Carry a bouquet of flowers into the kitchen on Tuesday. Or on every Tuesday. Carry the light of your own soul and let it shine, shine, shine.

Cause

Cause some kind of a stir.
Cause a ruckus.

When you enter, **cause excitement** to ripple through the room. When you're feeling mischievous, **cause some confusion.** Cause the entire group to burst into laughter; an instant later, cause them all to burst into tears. Pay special attention to anything or anyone who causes your heart to flutter. Pick your causes carefully, then **cause an uproar.** Say just enough to cause them to reconsider. Cause them to wonder if they really heard what they think they heard. Learn the law of cause and effect and learn that it can be broken. **Cause a confrontation.** When they ask you why you did, meet their gaze and say *Because.*

Celebrate

Celebrate anything you want. Celebrate the start of something, the end of something. If you're still going after five years or ten years or twenty-five years, celebrate. When your daughter starts her period, throw a quiet party to honor her passage into womanhood. When you stop yours, throw a raucous party in honor of your passage, too. String paper chains and hand-deliver invitations and bake a cake and break out the good stuff. Celebrate! Dance and sing, give speeches, take pictures, finger paint, play word games, and cut out cookies with sprinkles. Unfurl flags and spread torn quilts on the lawn and squeeze your own lemonade and bake a pie. Celebrate all the old holidays, and dream up a whole new batch of your own. Celebrate early, celebrate late, and celebrate often. Celebrate!

Challenge

Challenge yourself.

Challenge your body by boxing, biking, ballet, bowling, or bending over. Challenge your mind with chess, with calculus, Chaucer, chemistry, crossword puzzles, Chinese poetry. Challenge your spirit at synagogue, at a sweat lodge, in silence, at the stupa, through sacrament, sacrifice. When you become complacent, create new challenges. Challenge yourself to be more compassionate, more genuine. Challenge yourself to be less of a judge, less of a critic. Throw down your own gauntlet and challenge yourself. Do something harder, deeper, farther, faster. Move on to more complex, more intricate, more strenuous, more intellectual. Challenge yourself to be more human, more authentic, to be all you truly are.

Once you've reached a new place, challenge yourself all over again.

Change

If there's something about your life you don't like, change it. Make a big change or a small one. Change into someone entirely new. Change the color of your hair. Strip yourself of old, tired patterns and change into a woman who's creating her own beliefs about herself and her world. Change the channel. (*You know what I mean!*) Change the way you've arranged those pictures on the shelf. Change the route you take to work. Change your morning routine and come downstairs *before* you get dressed. Change newspapers. Change radio stations. Be brave enough to change your views on choice, on immigration, on capital punishment, on gun control. Change churches, change schools, change banks. Change toothpaste. Start making changes from the inside out, and when those around you cry *Change back!*, refuse to change your tune.

Channel

Create outlets for your energy so you don't
implode. If you're burning with passion,
channel that inner fire into outer expression.
Art works, cooking works, gardening works,
sex works. Same with music, writing, sewing,
rearranging rooms, building a table, running
a business, designing. If you're crawling the
walls like a pent-up beast, channel your physical energy before it destroys you and those
around you. Running works, lifting weights
works, swimming works, aerobic dancing
works, walking works, jumping rope works.
Learn to move energy up from the earth and
down from the sky and out in a safe and useful direction. Channel your anger, channel
your joy, channel the life energy that's flowing
through you. Channel through your fingers,
your toes, your voice. If your energy doesn't
flow, you can't grow.

Charm

Charm your way into a theater seat when the show has been sold out for weeks. When the police officer is about to write you a ticket, disarm him with your charm. Charm 'em with chutzpah, charm them with honey. Make your way to the front of the line and charm everyone in your wake. Charm a refund out of the store manager after two clerks and a supervisor said you never would. Charm a free dessert out of the waitress, charm three extra fried green tomatoes out of the chef. Be smart enough to know what charm is and what it's not. Forget about Prince Charming and crown yourself the Queen of Charm. There's never any harm in a little bit of charm.

Chat

Proudly exercise your right to make insignificant small talk. Sit under a tree or at a table or counter or in a car, and just chat. For that moment, forget about all the weighty issues of the world. Chat with another woman about practically nothing at all. Your hair. Your shoes. The interesting person who took your order at the coffee shop. The time you were thirteen and oh, you know. Chat easy, chat light. Chat about other people (it's not gossip, it's examining the human condition). Chat about something you read, but don't analyze too deeply. Chat about something you heard—but resist the temptation to compare and contrast. This time, don't network, don't interface, don't brainstorm. Just chat. About this, about that, just chat.

Check

Check in with yourself: how are you feeling, really? Check it out. Check in with your neighbor, just to make sure everything checks out all right. Take your best friend and check into a quiet bed-and-breakfast for a three-day weekend. Check your computer, your beeper, your watch, your calendar, and your brain at the door. Regularly, check your breasts for lumps. Check that mole to see if it's doing anything weird. Check your messages, and if that snippy synthesized voice tells you that you don't have any (again!), ask her *What makes you so smart?* Check out that good-looking guy in the four-wheel drive at the gas pump, and check out how he's checking you out while you check the oil. After a day in the woods, check for ticks. If someone puts you in check, check your position and *Checkmate!*

Chill

Cool down, girlfriend!

Take time out and chill. Pour yourself a cold lemonade, a cold soda, or a cold beer. Take a cold shower. Strap on an ice pack. Plug in an electric fan if you have one; stick your head in the sink if you don't. Count to ten before you let fly. Okay, count to twenty. Take a time-out. Or two. Breathe way deep—and don't forget to exhale. Walk around the block. Okay, run. Take a moment to decide if you're really ready to melt down and take everybody with you. Play some cool jazz, eat some cool food. Don't deny your fire, don't put it out, don't stuff it back in. Learn the power of a controlled burn, protect yourself from your own flash point, and know when and how to chill.

Choose

Every moment of every day, choose. Choose to do the right thing, the tough thing—not the familiar, easy thing. Choose the way of the warrior or the way of the coward. Make your choice out of love instead of fear. Choose from the heart. Choose to live fully, not to sleepwalk through your life. Choose to respond with the way you *really* feel, not the way you're *supposed* to feel. Choose the mineral water over the soda; choose the lemon juice and olive oil over the blue cheese; choose the walk in the park over the ride to the mall. Choose simplicity over extravagance. Choose conversation over the television. Choose to talk things out rather than stew in your anger overnight. Choose compassion and generosity. Choose to smile instead of frown. Make your own choices in your own time and choose to stick with them.

Circle

Be aware of circles and cycles. Make endings
into beginnings, make outsides into insides.
Arrange your favorite things into a circle—
stones and shells you picked up at the water's
edge, something shiny your grandmother gave
you, the doll you carried when you were six.
Form a circle with other women. Wrap your
arms around each other's shoulders and get
close enough so that your hips touch. Step
slowly to the right, to the left. If you see a
merry-go-round, ride it with your eyes closed,
now open. Hold your next meeting in a circle
so no one is in front and no one is in back.
When you're flying high, circle the airport sev-
eral times before you're ready to land. Learn
the difference between running around in circles and spiraling your way through the wheel
of life. One way holds you hostage, the other
sets you free.

Claim

Claim your rightful place, the place that has carried your name for all time. Claim your right to be honored as the earthly goddess you are. Claim your right to be loved for yourself alone, without strings and with a deep richness of soul. When you are questioned, claim the truth. Claim your innocence. Claim that which is rightfully yours and no one else's. Claim your own song. Claim your true path and make it yours. Claim you didn't know, if you didn't. Claim you were momentarily unaware, if you were. Claim your seat at the table, your place in the circle, your position at the dance. Claim your freedom. Claim the moon made you a tad crazy and the night song of the tree frogs didn't help. Claim your power, take it into your hands and up through your feet, and let it mingle with the awesome power of the Earth Herself.

Clear

Clear yourself for takeoff. Clear out your attic, your basement, that forbidden zone under the overhang where unspecified clutter has bred for eons. Clear the excess stuff out of your room so you can clear the excess stuff out of your head. Trim that hair in your face so you can see the world clearly and the world can see clearly who you are. Clear up your debts, be they financial, emotional, legal, or karmic. Clear a path through that overgrown field so you can get to the raspberries without getting scraped. That ancient argument, that silly misunderstanding, the whole brouhaha about the ink stain on the sweater: clear them up once and for all. Clear yourself of inner muck and junk, of toxic behavior and self-defeatism, of your anger and rage. Is that clear?

Climb

Go higher than you ever thought you could. Climb the ladder of success, whatever that is for you. Climb your way to the top. Take as long as you need: no one is watching the clock (except maybe you). Before you reach out to hold onto something or somebody, make certain it's strong enough to support you. Grit your teeth and scrape your knees and bleed and sweat. If your mountain is simply to get through the day, then scale it. When you get to the top, look back at what you've accomplished. Now smile or holler or cry. Before you head for the valley and the *next* mountain, remember the women who have gone before you and the ones who will follow your climb.

Close

Close the door quietly when you leave. *Please, for the one-hundredth time, close the refrigerator while you make up your mind.* Close one chapter completely before starting another. Hold a closing ceremony when you end a relationship. Create symbols and rituals that work for you. Perhaps burning a picture, burying a toy, hanging up loose ends of ribbons or yarn and tying them off with the help of some friends. Remember that when you close one door, another opens. So don't hesitate to close doors. Close the barn door *before* the horses escape. Close your presentation with a bit of inspiration, close your letter with a kiss. Close your day with a word of thanks and a quiet moment of reflection.

Collapse

Give in and admit that you just can't hold it all together anymore. Fall limp into a pair of waiting arms and let somebody hold *you* for once. Sob uncontrollably and shudder and let your eyes close and feel your body melting. Collapse into the rabbi's arms and tell her you want to come to temple. Collapse on a friend's sofa and ask her to make you a cup of tea. Collapse into a circle of women and know they will not let you fall. Collapse into the strong and comforting lap of the Goddess, of God, of Jesus, of Buddha, of an ancient Grandmother whom you never met yet know all the same. Take off your shoes and stockings and collapse on the floor. Find a big, warm bosom—real or imagined— where you can lay your head down and rest. Let go and feel the tension drain out of every muscle, every cell of your body. Believe that you're still competent, still strong, still capable, but for the moment, it's okay, you're safe now, collapse.

Color

Borrow some crayons from a child. Pick your
favorites: magenta, midnight blue, burnt
sienna, black. Color your hair if it makes you
feel better. Color it purple or blue or orange.
Color a design on a piece of fabric. Color eggs
when it isn't Easter, color the tops of cookies
when it isn't Christmas. Color your nails.
Don't stop there. Color your toenails. Color
the screws and nuts and bolts in your tool
box. Color the sidewalk with chalk, color your
walls with whatever shade you please. Color
your salad with red cabbage, radicchio, golden
bell peppers. Appoint yourself keeper of the
colors, and do your job exceedingly well.

Comfort

Comfort another.

Offer your hand in comfort, your heart, your home. Sing a quiet, comforting song, play a soothing melody. Comfort with words, with silence, with a loving touch. Trace a lazy circle on the cheek of a crying child. Stroke gently across the forehead of a laboring woman. Hold the hand of a dying man. Simply be present and you will know what to do. Prepare tea, cook up a pot of soup, toast up two slices of cinnamon bread. Pull the curtains and dim the lights. Draw a hot bath with rosemary oil. Fluff up a pillow, smooth out a blanket, fill the hot water bottle. Light a candle, massage and rock and hum and hold, and do nothing but be utterly human. Know that the sweetest comfort you will ever receive is the comfort you so freely give.

Commemorate

Commemorate the day you were born, the day your mother died, the day of the accident. The anniversary of the day you walked out, the anniversary of the day your beloved walked in, the anniversary of the day the twins were found. Your graduation, your ordination, your commission, your tenure. The month you lost the baby, the week you lost the house, the year of the earthquake. The big one. That horrible summer you lost six friends to AIDS. That wonderful summer you didn't lose any. Your youngest off to kindergarten, your oldest off to college. Plant a tree, bake a cake, light a candle, say a prayer. Commemorate these human passages, for, taken together, they mark an extraordinarily human life.

Commit

Some time in your life, commit to
something. A person, a place, a prin-
ciple, a profession. Decide to stick
with it through thick and thin. Give
it your very best shot and a whole lot
more. Commit for a year, or commit
for life. Commit to staying for as long
as it takes. Make a commitment to
something that matters to you. Make
a commitment to living your own
truth. Commit to a simpler lifestyle;
commit to quality, not quantity. Commit to building a
future with another person. (Make
certain you get a commitment in
return.) Commit to memory one
poem, one verse, or two facts that
will help shape the rest of your life.
Before you commit to anything,
commit to three days of reflection
and three nights of dreams.

Compliment

Compliment other women so they can know how magnificent they are. Say *You look lovely today. You have a nice, quiet energy about you. You are an inspiration.* Compliment a woman on the way she conducted herself in the meeting. Say *I like the way you pressed for an answer without being pushy.* Compliment her on her children. *Your son is a wonderful young man. I enjoy talking with him.* Compliment her on the way she cracked the tension with a humorous remark, on the way her eyes shine, on the smooth and easy way she moves. Compliment her on her strength *and* her vulnerability; her tenacity *and* her willingness to let go; her personal power *and* her humility. Compliment her very way of being exactly who she is, and know that she's a reflection of exactly who you are, too.

Concede

Give it up and let another person reap the glory. With grace and sincerity, concede. Concede that **no one is to blame,** but that it just isn't working out. Accept that she beat you fair and square. Concede that his arguments swayed the jury. Concede the race. Acknowledge that you were close, but she was closer. Concede the election. Yield to the decision of the judges or to the fates **or to the universe.** Know that you gave it your all, that you did your personal best. (If you didn't, reflect upon why not.) Be disappointed, be sad, be tearful, but **just let it be.** Leave resentment and envy behind. Concede that it's over and, **when you're ready,** go for it again.

Conceive

Give life to something—*anything*—until it's ready to be born. An idea, a dream, a baby, a book, a sculpture, a business. Be pregnant with something—*anything*—of your own creation. Hold it inside and feed it and love it and grow it until you're ready to share it with the world. Nourish it with your own breath and the warmth of your own body and the beating of your own heart. Conceive alone or with others or with the universe or with angels or with your computer. Carry your conception in a safe place for as long as it takes. A month or nine, a year or two or seven. When it feels like you can't carry it another day, wait a day and then release it. Let it come out in its own time, in its own way. Be prepared to feel the pain. Be prepared to feel the joy. Be prepared never to feel the same again.

Confess

Own up to it. Tell them it was you all along.
You were the one who left the secret notes,
the daily flowers. Yours was the car that
took out the corner shrub. It was so long
ago, tell them, and you were scared, tell
them. Take credit for your good deeds and
your not-so-good. Tell her it was you and
you just didn't have the nerve to tell her.
Don't keep them guessing any longer.
Confess your feelings, the ones you've kept bot-
tled up for so long. On an early morning
walk, when the mist is still rising off the
lake, confess your desire to chuck it all and
start over. Tell your truth: that you feel
there's something different for you to do,
something more meaningful. Tell them the
game has grown too old for you and you
for it and stop playing it now, and confess.

Confide

Confide in another human being. Tell her your deepest, darkest longings, your most secret joy. Know at least one person you can confide in. Confide your fears—of being carried away by an eagle, of living out your days lonely and unloved, of scaring them all away with your immeasurable power. Confide that you've always really, really liked Cher. Confide that sometimes you're confused about feminism. Sometimes you're confused about everything. Confide that you have a drinking problem. That your partner has a drinking problem. That you're frightened. Let someone trust you enough to take you into her confidence—and trust enough to take her into yours.

Confront

In the dark night of your soul, confront your greatest fears. Come face to face with your demons and demand to look them straight in the eyes. Confront the truth, no matter how unbelievable it may seem. If you have been living with inner beasts that torment you, confront them. If you have suffered at the hands of inner critics and inner judges and inner tyrants, confront them. Confront your outer critics, too. When you are ready, and if you so choose, confront your abuser. If you feel prepared, confront your attacker. Confront the fact that you may need a skilled professional to guide you every step along the way. Confront yourself in the mirror each morning, and you'll be better equipped to face life every day.

Connect

Do nothing else. Connect. Send
silver strands of light from your
heart to all those you love. Do
the same to those you love less.
Connect with people over beer
and pizza. Next time, hold the
pizza, hold the beer. Connect
without talking. Or ask enough
silly questions that you discover
the connection. Feel the unmistakable attraction to the person
who grew up in your hometown.
Who once visited the same ancient ruin in the same
month as you. Who also feels not-
quite-at-home here on Earth. Sing
together, laugh together, lie in the
grass and look for shooting stars
together. Find the connection that
transcends race and religion and
relationships. Don't ask why it does,
just connect.

Control

Control that control thing, okay? Get it under control. Your need to be in charge, to have the last word, to always, always have it your way and no other. Don't try to control others; don't allow others to control you. Let chaos rule now and then. Let your hair down; let your defenses down. Get that look of perfectly sculpted, perfectly manicured control off your face. Let it drop. Let the mask drop. If you're not driving a car, lose control once in a while. Be a little louder, a little funnier, a little sexier, and a lot more fun. Let somebody else call the shots for a change. Control your desire to control before it controls you.

Cook

Boil, bake, stir, stew, simmer, roast, reduce.
Cook for your friends, for your family, for the
widow down the hall. Cook for yourself. Fill
the air with garlic, with onion, with jalapeño,
lemongrass, basil, miso, mustard. Cook savory,
cook sweet, cook sour. Cook in the early morning on a hot summer day. Cook primitive over
a fire, cook gourmet on an overpriced stove.
Measure, don't measure. Cook because it's art,
because it's creative, because it's life. Cook to
Mozart, to McCartney, to Gabrielle Roth.
Cook naked—but watch for splatters. Bustle
around the kitchen and spill a little now and
then and clang pots and pans and drop a little.
Cook what your grandmother cooked and what
she never would. Now and then, forget about
fat-free, sugar-free, cholesterol-free, and cook
100 percent, unadulterated guilt-free.

Correspond

Write to someone
so someone will write to you.

Write long, newsy letters in longhand on hand-made paper. Ask her to write back. Share your ideas, your poetry, your fears, and include your favorite comic strip of the week. E-mail your emotions and request a response. Correspond every day for six weeks. Every month for twenty-seven years. Send pictures, send news clippings, send scribbled notes you've collected in a basket near your bed. Ask him to keep writing. Correspond when you'd rather talk, so you'll have something to read when you'd rather listen. Write fancy, write plain. Write on the back of computer paper, on yellow legal pads, creamy white stationery, note cards with dancing ducks. And always, always, remember to write back.

Council

Come together and sit and talk and listen and decide. Call women and men to council in a circle. Pass a talking stick or a talking stone so that everyone has an equal chance to speak. So that everyone can hear. Raise questions and present problems and pose solutions together. Take in the experience of every heart and the wisdom of every mind without judgment. Council with others when you're confused, when fear or conflict or tension fills the air. Council for peace. Council when there are visions to be shared and futures to be shaped. Council with your family, your friends, your coworkers, your community. Council with your adversaries. Council for as long as it takes. Council with deep respect for every voice and an open space for every truth.

Count

Count your blessings. If you get up to three or five or ten or twenty, count your blessings. Count up your possessions and consider whether you really need them all that much. Make every day count and don't take a moment for granted. Count to ten before losing your temper. If you can't count on people anymore, find other people you can count on. Start to count how many stars are in the sky—and count on getting lost in the awesome majesty of the heavens. Count yourself fortunate if you have a home. If you can't count all your marriages on the fingers of one hand, consider staying single. When you walk down the street, count how many people are smiling. Don't count on needing a calculator.

Create

Create something from nothing. Create a lovely home that's a reflection of your inner self. Create a business that offers quality service, and create a pay scale that women can actually live on. Create something with your hands. Use clay, wood, stones, wool, felt, nails, food, flowers, paint. Create the family you've always yearned for and include anybody you want. Create a wall hanging out of all those bits and pieces you've collected over the years. Create jewelry out of just about anything. Create a garden the butterflies will adore. Create exactly the kind of neighborhood in which you want to live. Create a very special ceremony when your cat is killed by a car. Create an altar that honors your creativity; create a life that honors itself.

Cry

Cry out when what you feel is too strong to hold in. Cry for help when you need it. Cry with your voice, your tears, with your actions. Cry because you want to, because it waters your soul and cleans out your dry and dusty places. Cry for the loss of old ways. Cry for every woman who was too tired to live and too scared to die. Cry for the children. Cry every time an old-growth forest on Earth is destroyed, never to return. Cry at what we've become and who we are becoming. Cry because you know we can do better. Cry out in frustration, in pain, in unbridled and relentless anguish. Cry because you're at a wedding—or because you're not. Cry the tears of all women, and know that you're crying your own tears, too.

Cuddle

Wrap yourself up in the warmest blanket you own. Jump into bed with whomever you love being close to the most, and tangle yourselves up, filling every nook and cranny and crevice with each other. Wear really soft slippers. Hold a teddy bear or a soft doll or a pile of towels just warm from the dryer. Nuzzle a shoulder, a neck; lay your head on a warm belly. Sink down into a nest of pillows until every muscle of your body is relaxed. Then turn over and around and let the pillows sink down into you. Climb into a tree and wrap yourself around a long, strong limb. Cuddle a person who is very young or very old. Tell yourself you're doing it for them, and do it for yourself.

Cut

Cut yourself some slack—at least as much as you cut others! Cut all your hair off and proudly proclaim *This is my face, world. Deal with it!* When the ties that bind are binding too tightly, cut them. Cut the cords and the apron strings that have become too restrictive. Cut them away from your neck, your hands, your feet. Create a ritual and tie knots in ribbons or yarn or string, and tie them all together in a big, knotted mess. Cut them apart with a knife, with scissors, with your teeth, with fire. Undo the knots, or bury them, or burn them. Make the cut symbolically, then make it for real. Cut the bull. Cut out a picture that helps your heart to soar, and put it on your refrigerator. Cut stars and moons out of shiny paper, and toss them around your room.

Cycle

Look for the patterns in your life, and honor them. Accept that every seven years you're ready for a new beginning. Acknowledge that jobs bore you after two-and-a-half years, and prepare for a change with excitement and a sense of discovery. Learn how you cycle every day, every week, every month, every year. Come to know how you change with your cycles and how they change you and those around you. Trust the rhythm of your cycles, no matter how different they are from the rest of the world's. No matter how out of sync you sometimes feel. Trust the power of cycles. A cycle will repeat itself again and again until you break the cycle for good.

Dabble

Live your life like an endless smorgasbord. Dabble in this and dabble in that. Dabble in the arts and dabble in the sciences. Dabble in cooking, in canning, in knitting. Dabble in real estate, in penny stocks, in futures. Dabble in bird-watching, old book collecting, llama breeding, stained glass window making. Try a bit of baseball, basketball, rugby, soccer. Sample solo living, co-op living, dormitory living, RV living. Dabble in living on the road and living on the edge. Dabble in metaphysics, in astrology, in psychic healing. Dabble in ancient history, in early music, in astronomy and biology. Dabble in dance. Dabble in rodeo. Dabble in bowling. Dabble in cyberspace and dabble in inner space, and leave plenty of space to dabble at dabbling.

Dance

Get up and dance. Let the heartbeat of the Earth move up from the soles of your feet and set your body into motion. There's nothing to learn but freedom. Step, shuffle, sway, bend. Dance on the floor, dance in your wheelchair. Dance with your hands, dance with your shoulders. Dance with yourself, dance with other women. Hold hands while you dance. Bump your behinds, bump your bellies. Let your eyes do the dancing. Dance everywhere, dance anywhere. Go to church and dance in the pews. Dance whenever you need to. Dance your anger, dance your joy, dance your indecision. Watch a belly dancer dance with a snake in sensual, fluid movements. Feel the energy crackle when a woman dances flamenco. Watch elders dance the old dances. Go to a play or a movie where everyone dances in perfect step with perfect legs and perfect precision. Go home, forget everything you saw, and dance your own dance.

Dare

Dare to make waves.
Dare to ask *Why?*

when no one else will. Dare yourself to walk into that restaurant alone. Dare to introduce yourself. Dare to be the oldest woman in the class. Dare to be the youngest. Dare to be happier than you ever thought possible. Dare to be different. Be *really* different! Dare to be as flamboyant, as brilliant, as sexy, as funny, as terrific as you really are. Dare to push your own envelope. Dare to push theirs. Dare to be first. Dare to suggest it's time for a change, then dare to lead the way. Dare to be vulnerable, dare to be real. Dare to proclaim *This is who I am*, and dare anyone to believe otherwise. Dare to claim your own power and to stand firmly rooted in your own truth. Go ahead, I dare you.

Declare

Right now, this minute, declare your freedom. Declare yourself a free and independent creature. Declare yourself *not for sale*, no way, no how. Declare your love to your partner, to your children, to the people you call family. Declare the time for change is upon us. Declare bankruptcy if it's the only way to get a fresh start. Declare loudly and proudly that henceforth, you will take your seat at the table. Declare your support for other women, for children, for elders, for the ones too often left behind. Declare your innocence, declare your devotion. Declare your intentions and when others follow your lead and start declaring theirs, think to yourself *Well, I declare!*

Decline

Graciously, gratefully, decline. Decline the nomination to be president of the board. (*I am so flattered, thank you, but I must decline.*) Decline when they volunteer you to head up the spring fund-raiser. (*How very nice that you thought of me, but I'm afraid I simply couldn't.*) Defer to someone else. (*Perhaps it's time for some new blood—I'm just not able to continue.*) Learn to decline when you're overcommitted. When it's the wrong thing at the wrong time or when you just don't want to. Decline the invitation without telling the whole, long, involved story. (*I appreciate your asking, but thank you, I won't be able to be there.*) Learn to say no. (*What a good idea; I'm sorry I won't be able to participate.*) It gets easier every time. (*Thanks, but I'll have to say no.*) Thanks. No. Sorry. No. I simply must decline.

Decorate

Decorate the canvas of your life. Make it a piece of living art. Decorate your home. Fill it with plants that breathe and mirrors that shine, prisms that paint rainbows on your walls and corals that remind you of the sea. Fill vases and jugs and bowls and baskets with feathers and flowers and fruit and anything that brings you joy. Decorate your body. Tattoo if you want to. Pierce if you prefer. Paint if that's your passion. Drape yourself with scarves that flutter and fly; with chains and beads of silver, gold, brass, and bone; with silken cloth, cotton, wool, embroidered and beribboned and as lovely as you. Decorate your garden with anything the squirrels won't eat, and decorate the sky with your smile.

Deepen

Go deeper. Deepen your capacity to love by loving more people more deeply. Deepen your understanding of your own psyche by reading about the goddesses Diana, Hestia, Aphrodite, Sophia. Deepen your knowledge of everything. Rely on every tool available to you. Deepen your ties to other women. Understand them more deeply, treasure their friendships more deeply. Know them in a deeper way. Deepen every relationship you have. Go to new levels of caring, of honesty. Deepen your willingness to risk. When you sink into the depths, go deeper into your own darkness and embrace it more deeply. Dive deeper into your own consciousness so you can mine the most precious jewels that lie deep within. Deepen your inner wisdom as you age, and your outer beauty deepens, too.

Defy Ignore them and do whatever you damn well please! Defy convention and wear what you want, love whomever you want, wherever you want. Turn a deaf ear to the media and the culture and the busybody down the block. Just say *No*. Go up against the odds, defy the naysayers and the dream destroyers and prove them wrong. Tell conventional wisdom to take a flying leap into an unconventional location where the sun never shines. Break rules that repress your freedom of expression and become more fully human in the process. Defy the doctors and live. Defy the accountants and prosper. Defy the lawyers and the politicians and the talk show hosts. Be willing to be ostracized for your defiance. Go to jail if you must. Lose everything you ever thought was important and revel in all that you gain.

Depend

Depend on others to make good on their promises. Depend on yourself to do the same. Depend on her to honor your agreement. Depend on him to tell the truth. Depend on yourself to learn the difference between codependency and interdependency. Be very clear about who you can depend on and who you can't. Don't depend on somebody else to clean up your messes. Create boundaries you can depend on, even when the winds are blowing. Entrust your most valuable ideas, hopes, secrets, and dreams to people you can depend on. Take a long, hard look at whom you're depending on these days—and for what. Take a person's hand in yours, look straight into their eyes, and say *I'm depending on you.* In the end, be prepared to depend on yourself if those around you prove undependable.

Die

Sometimes, part of you must die so that other parts can live. Let the controller part of you die, and you'll be able to trust and receive more. When the overbearing part of you dies, a softer, more compassionate you will thrive. Let the natural cycle of life, death, and rebirth be your guide. When your overarching need to do, to achieve, to produce is allowed to die, only then will you be able simply to be. When you are ready to let go of an old pattern that no longer serves you, it is a good day to let it die. Honor the passing of any part of yourself, for it has helped shape who you are becoming. Acknowledge your loss, mourn the dying, and turn to embrace the birth of a new and healthier you.

Dig

Dig in the earth and feel the moist soil teeming with life. Dig in the sand and discover where the glowing warmth meets the cool dampness. Dig deep for answers: push past layer upon layer and dig down until you strike the gold of your own truth. Dig a hole and bury your tears. Dig a grave and bury the robin you found at the side of the road. Dig a hole just deep enough to plant the seeds you want to flower and blossom in your life, but not so deep you fall into it time and time again. Dig for treasure wherever and however it's buried. When you feel you've exhausted all your strength and all your courage and all your compassion, dig deep and discover how much further you can dig.

Dinner

Dinner out, dinner in. Dinner by candlelight, dinner by moonlight, dinner by lantern light. Dinner out of a simple wooden bowl, dinner on a set of matching china. Dinner silver, dinner stainless, dinner with your hands. Dinner ordinary, dinner out of this world. Dinner French, Mexican, Cantonese, Indian, Thai, or West African. Dinner sushi. Dinner with reservations, dinner on the spur of the moment. Dinner at a big round table with boisterous conversations, dinner at a long wooden table in meditative silence. Dinner in your room. Dinner enough to get you through the night but not so much that it keeps you up all night.

When dinner's over, dinner dishes.

Discern

Practice conscious intolerance. Decide which people you want to spend time with, what relationship you want to invest in. Know the difference between truth and hollow flattery. Respond accordingly. Determine whether, this time, the out-and-out truth is what truly serves. Figure out whether you're being guided or led astray. You decide. Take an extra moment. Make them wait. What does your gut tell you? What does your heart tell you? Trust your inner ability to know what's right for you and what isn't. Learn the difference between the ways that fear and exhilaration move through your body. The surge you feel when you run away from danger is not all that different from the surge you feel when you're getting ready to reach the top of a mountain, birth a baby, win a race, celebrate an inner victory. Learn the difference. If it isn't *YES!*, it's probably *no*.

Do

Do what you want.

Do what makes you feel good.

Do the very best you can.

Do the right thing.

Do unto others as you would have them do unto you. Do something different today. Do something you never thought you would do. Do it up. Do your nails on the train (*do* ask your seatmate to stop staring). First be who you really are; then it's easy to do what you're supposed to do. Believe with all your heart that you can do it. Gather around you others who believe that you can do it, too. Do it your own way. Do your own thing. Don't do too much. Do a few things and do them well.

Don't try to do everything: it will do you no good.

Doodle

When you're bored, doodle. While the senator drones on and on, draw her nose thirty-seven different ways. When the service no longer serves you, practice writing your signature. Practice autographing your latest CD. If you're just a little nervous, doodle in the margins of your newspaper. List every lover you've ever had or wanted to have. If you have a lot of space left, list every episode of "Seinfeld" you've ever seen. List all the places you want to visit in the next year. Add up exactly how much you think it's going to cost. Doodle shapes. Triangles and stars. Cubes and yin-yang symbols and pentagrams and peace signs. Doodle spirals. If you're really nervous, doodle in the same spot so hard that you doodle right through the paper. *Sing Polly Wolly, doodle all the day.*

Draw

Draw your own boundaries and draw the line when someone tries to step over them. Draw all the drapes and hang out naked for the day. Draw with charcoal, with colored pencils, pastels, lipstick. Draw the moon and the stars on your face when you're feeling celestial. When you're feeling lucky, draw the winning ticket. Draw one card to an inside straight. When you draw the short straw, deal with it. When you sense things are drawing to a close, slip away gracefully. Once in your life, have a caricature drawn of yourself. Draw down the moon, draw a circle of white light to protect you from harm. Draw silly pictures on the sidewalk with chalk and hope that it never rains again.

Dream

Give yourself
over to the dream
time. Sky-swim, moon-bathe,
cross the threshold of every day into a
world where everything is possible and
anything can be yours. Dream your way into the
life you truly want to live. See it in your mind's eye:
what you're wearing, what the weather is outside, how
you feel, whom you live with. Sprinkle the dream with
prayer and song until it becomes your waking reality.
Build your dream into an altar, into a dress that sparkles,
into a picture that you hang on the refrigerator door.
Carry your dream close to your heart, share it only
with those you can trust to honor it. Dream it while
you sleep, while you wake. Dance into your
dream. One day, when you wake up, your
dream may have just come true.
When the dream changes,
dream anew.

Drive

Drive across the desert at twilight; drive down the coast at dawn. Drive every one of them wild with desire. Drive them all crazy. Drive the bumper cars, get all confused, and drive around in circles. Drive at least halfway across the country at least once in your life. Drive a car, a truck, an RV, a motorcycle, a backhoe, a bus, a van. Drive a brand-new Jaguar, even if it's just around the block. Give a cyclist a break and don't drive on the shoulder. Go to another country where you can drive on the other side of the road. Drive as if your life depended on it. When you find yourself driven to excess, slow down before you drive yourself over the edge.

Drop

Drop the act already! Drop your armor and be vulnerable. Just drop it to the floor. Once in a while, drop your defenses and yield. Drop your shoulders and drop your jaw so your energy can drop down into your belly where it belongs. Drop your pretenses and be real. Drop your masks and shrouds and veils and whatever else you've been holding up in front of you for so long. Drop anything and everything that gets between you and your truth. That gets between you and other human beings. When others just don't get it, drop a few hints. Drop a bombshell. When you're ready to drop from exhaustion, drop to your knees and ask for help. You never know what—or who—might drop from the sky.

Dry

Wash your hair and dry it in the morning sun. Dry your sheets on the clothesline whenever you possibly can. Hang your underwear on a tree branch to dry. Pick flowers all summer, hang them upside down in bundles of purples and pinks and yellows and whites, and dry them for winter bouquets. Dry fresh herbs for soothing teas and salt-free cooking and potpourris brimming with the aroma of the out-of-doors. Dry fresh sage or cedar or sweetgrass; bundle it with colored strings and burn it to purify your home and yourself. Take your sweaters outdoors to dry on a crisp autumn day. If you haven't got a tissue, dry your tears with the back of your hand.

Ease

Instead of thrusting your way out into the world, ease into it. Ease into a new job; you don't have to knock their socks off on the first day. Ease into a new relationship; you don't have to take your socks off on the first date. Get out of your own way and let things take their natural course. Ease your mind. Make the phone call, drop by to check in, go home and make sure you turned off the stove. There's no dishonor in taking the path of least resistance. Ease into a new rhythm. When you head off in a new direction, ease into it. Take things as they come and everything will be easier. When you see a woman struggling, offer to ease her way. When you see yourself struggling, ease up on yourself. If you're starting to lose control, ease up on the pedal and ease yourself back into the driver's seat.

Eat

Break bread together, share meals together, feast and potluck and dine and wine together! Cover the table with your salads and your pastas, your tricolored casseroles, herb muffins, homemade chili, watermelon, grapes and ice creams and yogurts. Feed each other big, drippy spoonfuls of lasagna, kimchee, fried chicken, borscht. Handfuls of key lime pie, rugelach just like your grandmother made, flourless chocolate cake, chocolate mousse, anything at all drizzled in chocolate. Taste everything together, and say *Mmmmm* and *Aaahhh* and *Ohhh* and lick your fingers and lick somebody else's fingers, too. Eat as much as you want—or as little—and know that there will always be *somebody* who really, truly, more than anything else, wants to do the dishes.

Embrace

Open your arms wide enough to hold close
everything that you hold dear. Open your
heart and wrap it around thirteen other hearts.
Now stretch it a bit further and embrace thirteen thousand hearts. Take in a new idea, a
new way of looking at things, and try it on for
size. Embrace it. Give your honey a squeeze.
Ask for one in return. Ask for lots. Sink into
every one. Hug from your shoulders to your
hearts to your bellies to your pelvises and
down to your toes. Feel the life force in yourself, in others, when you embrace. Hug someone who never expected it—yet who needs it
all the more. Embrace the totality of who you
are. Hug your wounds, your tender spots.
Embrace those parts of yourself you thought
you could never, ever touch. Drink them all in
with your deepest, most gentle embrace.

Emerge

Come out of the shadows and come into your own. Leave behind your armor and your shells and your veils and your protection and emerge fresh and newly born. Today, step from behind your screens and masks. Peel away the layers upon layers of fear and emerge into a world of love and trust. Emerge in your own time, in your own way, with your chosen guides at your side. See the world through the eyes of the woman you were always destined to be. Like a tiny chick cracking her way out of a darkened egg, emerge. Like a radiant butterfly, like a glorious rose opening from a tightly closed bud, emerge. Out of your past and into the gift that is your present, emerge. When it's time, when you're ready, emerge.

Empower

Empower yourself to take full and complete
charge of your life. Reclaim the personal power
that you never should have lost in the first
place—and come to know that you never really
did. Feel the breadth of your own power: the
power to feel deeply, the power to trust your
own voice, the power to create and bring forth
life. Learn the true meaning of power: how to
use it and not abuse it; how to stand in your
power without stepping on anyone else's. Join
with other women to empower each other. Sum-
mon up the inner will to co-create meaningful
and joy-filled lives. Empower yourself to take
control of your financial life and to prevent others from taking control of your emotional life.
Remember: you have the power to empower,
and anyone who tries to tell you otherwise has
absolutely no power over you.

Empty

Pour it out. Dump it out. Throw it out. Empty every bag,
box, and bureau. Empty every closet, every corner, every
cupboard, every cell. Pull it out. Drag it out. Clean it
out. Clear it out. Spread it out, sort it out. Look at
what you've collected, what you've stored, what
you carry around with you every day of your
life. Empty out the old, the unwanted,
the unusable. Empty out the pain, the
heartache, the memories. Empty
everything that offers nothing.
Leave things empty for a
while. Feel empty. Feel the
lack. Feel your way
through the
nothingness,
until at last
you feel
ready to
fill.

Enchant

Once in a while, when it's totally appropriate, enchant someone. A man. Another woman. The group sitting at the next table. Enchant with your voice, giving it lilt and just a hint of mystery. Say something in French. Or Italian. If no one understands, so much the better. Enchant with your eyes, at once provocative and conspiratorial. Let them twinkle. Enchant with your smile, with fingers that flutter like the wings of a dove. Enchant someone by floating across the floor, by sitting beside an open window and conversing with the stars. Be the enchantress who brings a certain something they can't quite define, who fills the room with mirth and magic, and who leaves them all a bit befuddled, entirely entranced, and touched by the goddess enchantment.

Endure

Go through the darkness and come out the other side.

When you think *I can't stand another minute of this*, know that you can. When you think *I won't make it through another day*, know that you will. When you can't take another moment of the pain and the fear and the feelings of hopelessness, take another moment anyway. Endure the heartache and come out heartstrong. Endure the tremors and the grief and the isolation and come out sturdy and robust and ready for another round. Like a diamond in the making, endure the heat and the pressure for what seems like eternity, and emerge with a new brilliance and clarity. When you think you've come to your end, dig deep and endure.

Engage

Engage fully in life.

No matter what you do, be present, hold your heart open and your mind will follow. Join a women's circle, a couples' circle, a neighborhood circle, a global circle. Talk to people, write to people, fax, e-mail, and page people. Share ideas and experiences with new friends, old friends, strangers. When something tickles you, laugh out loud. When electricity runs through a crowd, catch the fever. Go to meetings and speak your mind. Listen to live music whenever you can—or perform it. Support local artists— or be one. Read, vote, comment, protest, question, participate. There are a thousand ways to engage in life. Just pick one. Get out of your chair and out of your house. Ask someone to give you a boost. Get engaged now—and be wedded to life!

Enjoy

Find the joy in everything you do.
Even if it's only a sliver. Enjoy making
a peanut butter and jelly sandwich.
Then enjoy eating it, taking small bites
and licking your teeth with your
tongue. Enjoy washing the knife, feeling the warm water run over your fingers. Enjoy spending time with people
or stop the charade at once. When you
have five free minutes, spend them in
joy. Drop one major stressor in your
life, and enjoy the freedom that brings.
Be seven minutes late to a lunch date
or a breakfast meeting and secretly
enjoy being tardy. Enjoy screwing up
now and then. Enjoy being "in joy."
Go for a joyride and spread joy
throughout the countryside.

As you give joy, you will live joy.

Enrich

Enrich the soil before sowing your seeds. Enrich
the life of a child with trips to the museum and
the opera, to farms and forests and fantasy realms.
Enrich your friendships with the right blend of
togetherness, apartness, sameness, and spontane-
ity. Enrich your soul with long, quiet moments of
contemplation every day. To enrich your capacity
to love, love others. To enrich your capacity to be
loved, do the same. Enrich your worldview: dance
a Balinese dance, eat a Scandinavian flatbread,
sing a Russian song of mourning, honor an
African hero. Enrich your own feminine spirit by
paying greater heed to the cycles of the moon, to
your own cycles, to the cycles of women around
you. Enrich the greater feminine spirit by being
with women, sharing the truth of women's ways,
calling in the mystery to reveal Herself to women's
hearts and eyes.

Enter

Enter a room so that people know you've arrived. Before you enter, take a deep breath. Don't forget to exhale. When you enter a new phase of your life, mark it with a ceremony. Leave your shoes off when you enter your bedroom. Enter into a new relationship with yourself: treat yourself with greater compassion; put yourself first more often. When life presents you with an opportunity the likes of which you never encountered, open the door and enter. If you're scared, enter anyway. When you enter a restaurant or theater alone, enter with the knowledge that you have as much right to be there as anyone in a couple or a group. When you enter a forest, pause for prayer. When you enter a room filled with beautiful women of all sizes, all shapes, all colors, all ages, and all persuasions, enter with a grin on your face and enter proud.

Envision

See it in your mind's eye. Where are you? What are you wearing? What's the weather? What do you smell? What do you taste? Who else is there? Envision the house you buy for yourself. Envision walking onto the stage and receiving the award. Envision coming home every day to someone with two legs or four legs or no legs. Envision the people at the bus stop being friendlier, saying *Hello*. Envision the most important people in your life being proud of you. Envision them saying so. Envision the kiss. Envision holding the check in your hand. Envision peace. Envision a nation of wanted children. Envision your own version of God, of Goddess, of Divine Spirit. Envision your vision evaporating, while a new earthly reality emerges to take its place. Envision your life first, then make it real.

Escape

When you start to feel like a rabbit in a leghold trap, escape. If your home feels like a prison with no way out, escape. Escape from a dull and boring routine that's slowly but surely killing your spirit. Escape from any job, no matter how lucrative, that holds your creativity hostage and demands you pay with your physical and emotional health. Find a way out. However you must, escape from the constant needling of people who live their lives under a perpetual storm cloud. Get away for an hour or two, for a month or three. If you must, leave the marriage. Or the country. If you must, leave everything behind. When you've served your time and are ready for freedom, pardon yourself, and then escape.

Exaggerate

Oh, go ahead and tell a fish tale every once in a while. Tell them you're nine years older than you are—and let them marvel at how young you look! Exaggerate when they ask how you broke your toe. Tell them it was a climbing accident in Nepal. Blow things up a bit so they're larger than life. Exaggerate about that little fling you had over Labor Day weekend. Fib a little, just for the hell of it, and don't look back for a moment. Tell them thirty-six people showed up (instead of fourteen), that the critics raved (when they actually politely approved), that you finished the marathon while it was still light. (Okay, who cares if it was the morning of the next day?) Let a little of the coyote spirit into your life. If it's the big picture that really counts, what's the harm in painting it a little bigger? Trust me! I've done it a million times!

Exercise

Walk, run, bike, jump, dance, swim, play. But don't stop there. Exercise your rights as a human being. Exercise your faith. Do it often, then do it again. Exercise your right to be treated with dignity, and help others to exercise theirs. Exercise your brain so it doesn't get flabby. Figure out a problem. Take a stab at a crossword puzzle, learn a new language. Better yet, learn an ancient language. Try to guess "whodunit" before the end of the show. Exercise your heart without ever getting on the stairs. Feel the burn when you love someone who seems not at all lovely. Stretch your heart muscle so it can open wider and stay open longer. Exercise your emotions by getting them in motion. Can you still cry when you see something tender? Are your lips toned enough to break into a broad smile at the sight of something sweet? Exercise your humanity: use it or lose it.

Experience

Do it, try it, feel it. Stop going through life as if it's some kind of virtual reality, and start living! Let an earthworm crawl up your arm. Sit with a dying person no matter how scared you are. Jump in the mud if you've always been clean; retreat in silence if you've always been boisterous. Eat Indonesian food. Camp. Take off your shoes and walk in a fountain. Lie down, belly to belly, on a moist patch of earth. Start singing when no one else is. Dance before anyone else does. Travel alone. Live together. Turn off that TV now! Work on a farm, hold a baby chick. Go into that cafe you'd never imagine going in. Smile at the woman next to you in line, and mean it. Experience a full-spectrum life and chalk it all up to experience.

Explore

Dive into deeper waters and chart the outback of your soul. Go where you've never gone before. Explore a new way of living as though it were a new continent. Discover its treasures. Explore what lies beneath the overgrown vines and inside the darkened caves and beyond the very edges of your horizon. Explore the awesome universe that has been placed at your feet. Start small and explore your neighborhood. Explore the nooks and crannies of your block. Explore friendships with women and men who seem totally alien to you. Explore how far you can go. Explore all your options, uncover all your possibilities. Investigate what works best and what doesn't work at all. No matter where you explore, you're certain to discover that the adventure never ends.

Express

Untie your tongue and untwist those knots in your belly. Let your feelings be known and don't hold back. Express yourself. If you're grieving, cry. If you're tickled pink, laugh and giggle and prance around the room. If you're angry, be so. Use words. Write them down, speak them, put them out for the world to hear. Call a talk show and express your opinion. Express your art. Use crayons, use clay, use your clarinet. Express yourself with your hands. Sign. Draw pictures in the dirt, finger paint, knit. Express your feelings for someone else. Write a song. Sing it. (Okay, you can tape it.) Pick out tiny gifts that express your love, your gratitude, your apologies, and send them off in tiny boxes and pouches filled with glitter and confetti. If you want them to arrive tomorrow, express them.

Face

Face the truth in its myriad forms. Face the mirror and really, really look at your own eyes, the shape of your own lips. Face another human being and let her eyes meet yours. Face your own limitations—especially if you believe you don't have any. Face the reality that life and death go hand in hand, that every expansion is followed by a contraction, that every winter eventually melts into spring. Face your accusers. Face up to your mistakes and resolve them as best you can. Face east and greet each day with gratitude. Face your own mother and see yourself where you can. If she's no longer here, face her in spirit. Face the fact that you can't give your child everything he asks for, and face the fact that he'll probably keep on asking. Face your dragons, face your demons. Once you get a good look, resist the urge to do an immediate about-face.

Fast

If you're eating too much too quickly, fast.
Fast completely for three days. Fast with
juice, fast with water, fast with a very few
select foods. Fast because you've gotten too
sluggish. Because you're feeling bloated all
the time. Fast because you've gotten too
slow. Fast to clean your insides out so you
can have a clearer view from the outside
in. Keep quiet when you fast, and listen to
what your gut says: that you've been swal-
lowing too much, that you've been taking
on so many new ideas that you can't digest
them fast enough, that you need to let go
of a whole lot of . . . stuff. If the idea of
fasting makes you say *Whoa, not so fast!*,
then start with a half-fast attempt.

Feed

Feed your soul whatever it craves. Long walks in the forest, long days at the seashore, long nights filled with sleeping or dreaming or skywatching or loving. Feed your creative juices. Feed them time, feed them space, feed them a rich diet of fantasy and friends and feelings. Feed your spirit. Feed on dance and song and prayer and ceremony. Feed on the energy of the circle. Feed yourself before you're starving, before you dry up. Feed yourself from a river that is pure and untainted, sincere and unadulterated, fresh and clean and flowing. Oh, and one more thing: don't forget to feed the baby, feed the cat, feed the fish. But first, feed yourself.

Feel

Feel the pain, feel the joy, until you feel you'll surely evaporate. Stop holding back from laughing with your belly, loving from the deepest places of your heart, swooning with the sensuality of life itself. Feel how good it feels to love another human—and if you're lucky, to be loved in return. Feel the warmth inside you when you do the right thing. Feel the fire that's ignited when someone tramples that which matters to you. When another's disregard or arrogance enrages you, feel the anger rise up and roar! Let your honest feelings come through, even the ones that make other people squirm. If you're not truly feeling, you're not truly alive—you're just going through the motions and getting nothing in return.

Fib

The check is in the mail. No, I never received your message; I guess my voice mail was down. The computer crashed just as I was finishing that spreadsheet. Gee, I'd love to come, but I already have plans. I had car trouble. Sorry, I have relatives coming into town that weekend. Oh yes, I had a really nice time, too. That dress looks great on you, really great. No, I don't think you were too aggressive. Too quiet. Too talkative. I really hope we can get together more often. Let's get together really soon. I'd like that. That sounds perfect. No, really, everything was perfect. Me, tell a little white lie? Fib? No, never, I've never done that before.

Fight

Have the courage to fight for what you know is right. Take off the white gloves and put on the boxing gloves. Fight tooth and nail on behalf of the children. Fight for the woman you never met who was raped and was then called a liar. Fight for the end of intolerance. Fight alongside women who just want to earn a livable wage. Who just want to stay at home and raise their children. Who just want to get through a day without fear of being beaten, shot, or killed. Fight for freedom everywhere. Support the battles of people who seem different from you—and realize they're not very different at all. Fight with your words, with your money, with your influence, or simply with your presence. Fight by clapping hands, by raising your hands in the air, by holding hands. Choose your fights carefully, fight to win, and fight to end the fighting once and for all.

Fill

When your cup is half empty, fill it. Fill your life with the things that fill your heart. Fill jars full of pennies or buttons or colored water or hard candy. Fill your home with plants and music and orbs that make dancing rainbows and good friends and good food. In the fall, fill a wooden bowl with acorns, with pinecones. Fill your favorite teacup with your favorite jasmine blend. Fill a box with things you don't need, label it *Free*, and set it out by the side of the road or leave it at a church or shelter. When a room is filled with tension, fill it with the warmth of your smile. Fill your arms full of puppies or kittens or babies or dolls or stuffed toys or sheets and towels fresh from the dryer. Turn off the electronic gadgets and fill your time with real conversations with honest-to-goodness people. Fill up another person's life with joy. When you fill up the car with gas, think about driving less. When you fill up your grocery cart, think about giving more.

Find

Find a way back. Find a way forward. Find your way through. Find lots of women whose company you enjoy and, in the end, find yourself. Find the missing link in your history, the one that explains your lingering sadness. Find out what makes you feel most alive, and then find ways to give it to yourself often. Find the real questions before you worry about finding the answers. Find a woman writer you adore and read everything ever written by her, for her, or about her. Find a stone shaped like a heart and keep it in your pocket. Find the truth behind people's hollow words. Find a new, healthier, more satisfying way to be in relationship with your lover. When you can't find what you're looking for, find the strength to keep on searching. Eventually, you'll find what you need.

Finish

Finish what you start. Finish up the last calculation, the last page, the last round, the last lap. Finish that final assignment so you can finish up your degree. Finish that vest you've been working on for eons, that tile job you thought you'd never finish. *Would someone please finish up this last bit of soup so I can finish up in the kitchen?* Finish that discussion when you're both feeling a bit calmer. Pray that they finish soon so you can go home. Finish sanding, finish trimming, finish cutting so you can put away the tools. Finish off one project before you start another. Let go of that relationship: it's finished. Let go of being a doormat: you're finished! Go back and finish what you swore you would never finish in a million years. When they ask how far along you are, say *I'm finished!*

Flirt

Flirt for fun and leave it at that. Flirt with
the man at the diner, the woman in the
video store, the couple looking at the gardening tools. Smile wildly, flash your interest, do some monkey business with your
eyes. Cock your head to one side and raise
your eyebrows and utter flirtatious remarks.
Drop an innuendo or two. Do something
provocative with your hair and your finger
and your mouth. You figure it out. Strike a
suggestive pose (and have some clear idea of
what you're suggesting). Flirt shamelessly,
brazenly, until everyone is flirting back. Let
them ask quizzically, *Is she flirting with us?*
Laugh in a lilting kind of flirty way, toss
out a little panache, a bit of *je ne sais quoi.*
Flirt until the flirting is done, then flit
away, leaving a flirtatious air behind you
and not one iota more.

Flow

Get out of your own way and let
your life flow with the grace of a
clear mountain stream. Stop
trying to orchestrate and manage
your way through life. Stop trying
to swim against the current; the
struggle will get you nowhere and
will exhaust you in the process. Flow
into and out of your days without
clinging desperately to worn-out ideas,
deadened hopes, lifeless relationships. Let
go and let flow. Spend time on the banks
of a river, creek, or waterfall. Feel the
serenity and ease of the effortless flow.
Remember how a stone that is
tumbled and carried by the flow
ends up smooth and polished
with no rough, ragged edges. Be
that stone and go with the flow.

Focus

Clear away the clutter, and focus. Concentrate on that which is before you and nothing else. When thoughts threaten to distract you, kindly send them on their way and regain your focus. With the precision of a laser, focus. Put down the newspaper and focus on the person talking to you. Turn off the television and focus on your reading. Close yourself off from unsolicited advice from people you neither trust nor respect, and focus on what *you* want. Focus on the sky, on the silent movement of clouds as they cover and uncover the sun. Sharpen your viewpoint on what's truly important—and keep everything else a blur. Focus on a single ant moving a single grain of sand, and marvel at her ability to keep her focus. Now, without losing focus, marvel at *your* ability to keep yours.

Fold

When the dealer deals you a lousy hand, fold.
Write little love notes, and fold them small
enough to slip into the most unlikely places.
Whip the egg whites and fold them in slowly.
Fold the clothes as if folding were a sacred ritual, a meditation. Fold slowly, with precision.
Line up cuffs and sleeves and legs and corners.
Crease with the side of your hand. Fold into
triangles instead of squares. Keep your spine
limber enough so you can fold into a ball and
roll around on the floor. When you're sitting
quietly, fold your hands and put them in your
lap. When the word has to get out fast, call
out for pizza and sit on the floor and fold the
flyers and stuff the envelopes until the job is
done. If your business just isn't making it, cut
your losses and fold. In time, you'll be ready
to unfold.

Follow

Follow your heart, even when your head says
No, follow me! Follow your hunches; why else
would you have them? Let another woman lead
so you can follow. If you want others to follow,
then lead! Follow a hawk as it swoops and soars
through the sky. Follow the path of a moth as it
seeks out the light, bumping and crashing even
while in its very glow. Listen to the wisdom of
that moth or of a stone or of a tree, and follow
the guidance you will be fortunate enough to
receive. Follow in someone's footsteps only
until you're ready to carve out your own. Follow your dreams without reservation—wherever
they take you. Pick a direction for your life and
follow it until you know it's time to follow
another. You will be given signs along the way;
you only need to follow them.

Forget

Sometimes, just remember to forget. Forget that you were told not to make waves. Forget that you were taught to be seen and not heard. Forget that some people still believe a woman should be barefoot and pregnant—and conduct yourself as though everybody knows better. Forget everything you ever heard about good girls not touching their own bodies. Or anyone else's, for that matter. Forget all the times they told you that you were too stupid or too plain or too clumsy or too smart or too "you know." Remember those women whose pictures are always on the magazine covers? Forget you ever saw them. Forget those awful memories of junior high school, and start creating wonderful new memories. Remember what's-his-name? Forget him! When someone tells you *I told you not to act like that*, smile and say *Oops, I forgot*.

Forgive

Experience the power of forgiveness.
Say *I forgive you*, and mean it. Forgive
everyone who ever wronged you. Forgive him for breaking your heart. Forgive her for telling everyone your
deepest secret. Forgive them both.
Stop holding grudges, and forgive.
Forgive yourself for being human, for
not knowing all the answers all the
time. Once and for all, for the sake of
your own sanity, forgive. Let the
sweet and simple rain of forgiveness wash over you.
Ask for forgiveness, offer forgive-
ness. Somewhere, find the inner
depth to forgive the man who
raped, to forgive the woman who
killed, to forgive the friend who
betrayed a loving trust. For life, for
love, for peace forever; for you, for
them, forgive.

Form

Form your own organization and form your own rules. Inform everyone that the format of the meetings will be strictly informal. Form your own conclusions, and let others form theirs. Never use the long form when the short form will do. Form a lasting friendship with someone you used to hate. Form a circle around the big, beautiful woman gyrating gloriously to the beat of the drum. Cheer her on wildly while you admire her round and magnificent form. Form lots of circles. Form a women's-every-other-Thursday-movie-discussion circle. Form a women's-quilting-and-cognac circle. Form a women's circle for women who have always avoided women's circles. Do your best to form more perfect unions, and when the form breaks down, reform.

Free

Free yourself! Free yourself from habits that suppress you, people that depress you, rules that repress you. Get rid of clothing that pinches, binds, or leaves red designs on your skin—and free yourself to move in comfort. Free up some time every week—or every day—to express your creativity. Free your mind of negative thoughts and belittling beliefs. Sell your house and free yourself from the never-ending world of home maintenance. Free yourself from draining relationships with people who want only to take and never to give. Cut up your credit cards and free yourself from the vicious cycle of debt and interest that never goes away. Free the poet that's locked inside you. Free the athlete who never got to run, the ballerina who never got to dance, the diva who never had the freedom to sing. Free yourself to be the woman you were always meant to be. And be free.

Fuss

Let me get you another pillow. No, really, it's okay. *Do you want caffeine tea or herbal?* Oh, anything is fine. *I'll sleep on the sofa, and you can have my bed.* Oh no, really, I love the sofa. *All I had was tuna, so I made a quick trip to the store.* Oh, really, tuna would have been great. *Is the light all right for you? Should I change the bulb?* Please, relax, it's perfect. *I made your favorite dessert. It took three hours, but I know how much you love it.* You're kidding! Really, a cookie would have been fine! *I did your laundry while you were napping.* You what??? *It was raining, but I went out and got your paper.* Please, don't fuss. *Would you like strawberry jelly or raspberry jam?* Oh, don't make such a fuss. *A fuss? Don't be silly! Who's making a fuss?*

Garden

Garden in the early morning, while the green leaves are damp and the sun is still low in the sky. Grow flowers, vegetables, bushes with berries, long, trailing vines that reach for the sky. Weed and water and wait. Weed out anything that seeks to strangle or crush a tender, young blossom. Dig. Dig deep. Deeper. Bury bulbs and believe they will bloom. Plant your seeds and know that, in time, you will reap your harvest. Kneel down in the soil. Put your hands in the moist and fertile earth. Go to the garden when you feel like nothing is growing anywhere else, when you fear that everything is dying. When you need to remember that everything is. Growing and dying, right here, all around, when you garden.

Gather

Gather an armful of flowers and cradle them close to your breast. Gather ye rosebuds while ye may. Gather your family around you before they're all gone. Before you're gone. Gather together for whatever ritual you please. Gather together with women and men you love. Sip tea together, walk in the woods together, talk and talk and talk, read aloud to each other, do absolutely nothing together. Revel in how your hair and your skin and your bodies and your stories are so different—and so utterly alike. Cook and eat together, stand beside the washing machine and cry and hug and wail together. And, most assuredly, laugh together until your sides ache and your pants are wet.

Gaze

Lower your eyelids halfway, and gaze in the direction of something that pleases you. Instead of penetrating with your eyes, soften your focus to see things in their true light. Gaze lovingly at the gentle curve of a handmade bowl, the way that sunlight filters through the old window in your attic. Gaze at a wildflowered hillside until you see just a splash of yellow here and a burst of magenta there. Gaze upon the face of an old woman with your eyes, trace the lines that travel around her mouth and circumnavigate her forehead. Read a bit of her history in her face. Let your softened eyes meet hers gently, and toss a quiet smile in her direction. Learn to see the unseen. Gaze at a skyscraper and see a temple. Gaze at the moon and see a woman with a basket. Gaze into the mirror into your own eyes, until your vision takes you past your own exterior and into the deepest recesses of yourself.

Gesture

Give a sign.

Gesture for someone to come closer. Now closer. Now, with the slightest turn of your hand and shake of your head, gesture for them to stop. Speak volumes without a word. As a gesture of kindness, invite a neighbor in for tea. As a gesture of forgiveness, send flowers. As a gesture of compassion, drop a note to the woman who lost her family, who lost her legs in that horrible accident, who lost all hope when her life's work was confiscated by the police. In a gesture of solidarity, stand alongside the picketers. Make the tiniest, quietest gesture, and see how far it ripples out into the world. How many people it touches. How powerful a simple gesture can be.

Get

Get real.
Get a life.
Get the life you always wanted to get.

Get all you deserve. Get there early and get the best seat. Get the ripest pear in the store and devour it as soon as you get to the car. Get sweet, sticky juice all over the seat. Get all of your work done early and get out the door not a minute too soon. Get it right the first time. Get up twelve minutes early and get in a little stretching. Get on the Internet before you get left behind. Get a higher return or get a new accountant. Get a lower deductible or get a new policy. Get happy. Get out a little more often. Get in a little reading before bed, then get to sleep early. Get angry, get over it. Get going. Get gone.

Giggle

You're never too old for a gay, girlish giggle. The kind that never grows to a full-blown laugh, tittering and teetering right on the edge. Do your best giggling in inappropriate places, at inappropriate moments. Giggle in class, in church, in the courthouse, or (Heavens!) at the Motor Vehicle Department. Giggle just when the bride is about to say *I do*. Giggle just before the deceased is lowered to her final reward. Try to stifle a giggle, but know that you never will. It's the nature of giggles to slip out between your lips, between your fingers, uncatchable and uncaring. Giggle when you make a mistake during the recital. Giggle at work, right there at your desk, when the vice president of marketing walks by. She'll glare and stare; you'll giggle and giggle. Hey, who's having more fun, anyway?

Give

Choose something you swore you could never, ever live without, and give it away. The ring you-know-who gave you long ago. Your dog-eared copy of *Women Who Run with the Wolves*. The plant that finally, finally bloomed after everyone gave it up for dead. Give it to a friend or, better yet, give it to a stranger. Give two hours every other Thursday. Give a gift to the woman who answers your phone. Make it small and totally unexpected, and remember to tie it with a curly ribbon. Give a talk that makes someone laugh. Makes someone cry. When the man comes to clean the carpets in your apartment before you move out, give him your beloved antique mirror so he can give it to his girlfriend. Once in a while, give yourself a gold star on the refrigerator door. Giving is the first act of living.

Go

Get going! Go your limit, then go some more. Go first or go last or go somewhere in the middle, but go already! Give yourself the green light and take off. Go a way you've never gone before. Go alone or with a partner, or go with a group. Go with someone different for a change. Go now, because it's time to go. Go tomorrow. Ask yourself why you haven't gone yet. Let yourself go. Let her go, let him go. What are you waiting for? Give yourself permission to go. Go down the path, go through the gate, go around the corner. Go into a room you've never gone into before. When you need privacy, go to your room. Better yet, tell everybody else to go to theirs.

You go, girl!

Grieve

Let yourself feel the pain of losing. Grieve
for a friendship that's over or a parent who
has died. Pour out the anguish that comes
with being fired from your job, laying a
beloved animal to rest, having your pride
and your stature and your belongings
stripped away from you. Feel how much it
hurts. Take absolutely as long as you need.
Cry and wail. Sob and fall to the floor if you
must; put everything else aside while your
tears flow. Scream and bang your fists
against something soft and cry out *Why?*,
knowing there isn't really an answer you can
wrap your brain around. Grieve for the loss
of a part of yourself. When you're empty,
when the grieving subsides, remember that
spring always follows winter and that every
time something dies, something else is born.

Ground

When you feel yourself floating
away into thin air, ground yourself.
Lie down and connect with the
grounding power of the Earth. Work
in a garden. Eat bread; eat rice. Put
your arms around a tree trunk; put
your arm around a human trunk.
Kneel down and place your head on
the ground before you. Get back
into your body with a walk, a run, a
hike. Feel long and strong roots
growing from the soles of your feet deep into the soul of
the Earth. Breathe slowly, and
make every breath complete.
Massage your legs and your hips.
Scrub a floor, cook potatoes, sit
in a chair and sew on buttons.
Stay close to the Earth; let gravity
do its thing, and when you feel a
solid peace within, you'll know
that you've been grounded.

Grow

Become more than you are right now. Grow into a greater sense of self. Grow in your capacity to listen, to love. Grow more deeply into your relationships. (Yes, all of them.) Admit that you're growing more beautiful with each passing day. Grow sunflowers in the front yard instead of grass. Grow peppermint, basil, cilantro on the windowsill in tiny pots or cottage cheese containers or beautiful old ceramic things. Grow into yourself. Catch up with the nose you always thought was too big, the heart that always seemed too open, the sexuality that seemed insatiable. Grow beyond all the walls and fences you thought were stopping you. Grow a garden that's alive and bright and luscious, multilayered and multitextured and filled with hardy perennials and showy annuals. Grow your own garden inside yourself, and tend it well and always.

Guard

Guard fiercely that which others want most to wrest from you. Your inner wild places and the freedom to visit them often. The gateways to your very soul, the keys to your secret garden and all that you cultivate therein. Guard against attacks of all sorts by those who covet your light and envy your brilliance. Create shields visible and invisible, and infuse them with the power to deflect invasions of your body, mind, and spirit. Guard the security of your home as if it were more valuable than the grandest place on Earth, for surely it is. Establish your personal boundaries and guard them against interlopers who would barge in against your will. Be the guardian of your own solitude and that of others, and peace shall always be yours.

Guess

Don't know? Guess. Not sure? Guess. Take a stab and guess. Lost your measuring spoons? Just guess. Filling out some insignificant form? Just guess. Guess how many shoes you've bought in your life. Guess how many you've given away because they hurt. Throw away your scale and guess your weight. Guess within ten or twenty pounds and leave it at that. When a friend asks you to be in her wedding, guess that you're going to have to shell out for a dress you hate. Guess you'll never wear it again. When the officer asks *Do you know how fast you were going?*, guess low. When your boss asks *How much of a raise do you think you deserve?*, guess high. When they ask *Are you absolutely certain?*, say *Yeah, well, I guess.*

Hang

Just hang. Ignore the list of things to do, ignore the piles and boxes of unfinished business, ignore the fact that everybody else is rushing around getting things done. Hang out with yourself; hang out with a friend. Hang around the house on a rainy day. Hang out at the library. When you feel the darkness come over you at every turn, hang in there and know that this, too, shall pass. Take your necklaces out of that box and hang them where you can see them every day. Hang as many bird feeders in as many trees and bushes as you can. Hang bells in the bathroom. Hang your favorite pictures all over everywhere, hang red ribbons from the branches of a tree, and hang a tiny angel over your door.

Harvest

Fill your arms with all the abundance you have
manifested. Harvest the fruits of your labor.
After planting the seeds of hard work and dedi-
cation, harvest your well-earned success. From
sowing the seeds of loving relationships, harvest
a lifetime of love in return. Bring home the tro-
phy, the signed contract, the check, the baby
you prayed for and searched for all over the
world. Pick up your diploma, throw your cap
skyward, receive your just reward. Go to your
mailbox and find the letter at long last. Pick up
the phone and hear them say *Yes*. After planting
your seeds and tending them well and standing
back and waiting and being patient and sometimes impatient, bring in the harvest. Be
accepted, be selected, get hired, reunite, make
the final cut, get paid, get recognized, receive
tenure. And while you're harvesting with one
hand, be sure the other is sowing anew.

Have

Have it your way. Have it all. Have a day off, have a ball. Have an absolutely unforgettable time. Have dinner out; have anything on the menu you want. Have a beer, have dessert first. Have great sex. Have an orgasm. Have a handful. Have a headache? Have an aspirin. Have a divorce, then have a second marriage that's better than the first. Have the most beautiful children on the face of the Earth. Have the shortest labor on record, have the longest. Have the original boss from Hell. When you have to, have a cow. Have a hissy fit. Have a conniption. Have a heart, have a brain, have courage. Have a clue. Whatever you do, have a sense of humor. Remember: the more you have, the more you have to give.

Heal

Woman, heal thyself. Once and for all, find
your emotional scars and psychic wounds and
set about healing them. Heal by talking, painting, acting, dancing, singing, cooking. Let your
heart lead you. Heal in solitude, in a group, in a
circle, in a community, in an ashram. Heal in
the forest or on a mountaintop, in a clinic or in
a church. Heal with a therapist, a shaman, a
counselor, a bodyworker, a priest, a priestess, a
rabbi, a minister, a doctor, a medicine woman.
Let your heart guide you. Heal while you're in
your thirties, in your forties, in your sixties, in
your eighties. It's never too early, never too late.
Start healing. Do it in 12 steps or in 235 steps or
in 1,200 steps. Heal with herbs, heal with meds,
heal with energy, heal with the power of prayer.
Heal others by healing yourself. Heal your com
munity by healing yourself. Heal the planet by
healing yourself.

Hold

Hold hands with anyone you darn well please. Whenever you have the chance, hold a baby, a puppy, a pillow in your arms. Hold your vision for three days before you share it. Hold a pussy willow up to your skin. Hold your tongue before you willfully shame or blame another or yourself. Otherwise, hold yourself to your own truth. Sound a note, and when it sounds as though it's coming from everywhere else but your own mouth, hold it as long as you can. Hold a salon in your living room and invite the most interesting people you know. Hold a sun-ripened strawberry in your hand for at least three-and-a-half minutes—then hold it on your tongue for a minute more. To have all that you desire, hold onto nothing at all.

Honor

Honor yourself for the fine woman you are. Honor women in every stage of their lives, be they young maidens, mothers, crones. Use the word. Say *I honor you for your courage* when a woman takes an unpopular stand. Say *I honor you for your openness* when a woman allows her emotions to flow freely. Honor the woman who has had a child—and lost it. Honor the woman who, by fate or by choice, will never have a child. Honor the woman who fought off an attacker with her bare hands—or did anything, including nothing, to stay alive at the hands of another. Honor the grandmothers who tell the stories, who remember the old ways, who have time for the young. Honor the woman who has fought to stop war—and the woman who has fought when war called her name. Honor the woman who cleans, who cooks, who serves, who governs, who grows, who defends, who protects. Honor the woman in every man, if you are lucky enough to catch a glimpse of her. Honor every woman as you would have every woman honor you.

Hope

Never give up hope. Keep alive that spark that keeps you going. Hope that they find a cure. Hope he can last that long. Hope that somehow, miraculously, they all survived. Hope you get accepted, hope you get promoted, hope they like your work. Hope that you're not pregnant. Hope that you are. Hope, hope, hope that the computer doesn't crash before you finish your thesis. Hope that your daughter has listened to a word you've said. Hope that you've said at least some of the right words. Hope there's rain enough for the crops, but not too much for the rivers. Against all hope, believe in hope.

Howl

In the dark of the night, howl at the moon. Howl in sync with the coyotes who line the ridge at dawn. Live your life like a wolf, and howl long and low, high and shrill, plaintive and wailing and ancient. Howl with laughter, roaring. Howl your grief. Howl your loneliness. Howl when you need help now. Sound a warning call that echoes through the canyons. Howl when the others are singing, when the others are weeping. Shriek and scream and growl and cry out when there are no words that touch deeply enough or sound wild enough. Howl a mournful, soulful, beautiful howl. You know how. Howl.

Hug

Hug people, a pillow, animals, trees, yourself. Full-body hugs, deep hugs, friendly hugs, jumping-up-and-down-with-joy hugs. Group hugs, circle hugs, lying-down hugs, hugs that go around and around and never seem to stop. Hug outside the market, in front of the church, in the swimming pool, at the scenic overlook, on the back porch by the light of a citronella candle. Hug on the way to the cemetery, beside the grave. Hug to keep from falling to the ground in grief. Hug when you can't quite find the words to say *I made it all the way. Thank God you're safe. She's terminal. We got the grant. The test was negative. They picked my design. I heard the baby's heartbeat. Poppa's coming home. We lost everything. I love you very much.*

Hush

Hush now. Quit explaining, stop discussing. Put an end to the talk, talk, talk, and hush. Breathe out slowly and feel the silence. Listen to everything, to nothing in particular. Rest your throat and your mind with a strong dose of hushed silence. When you've said enough, hush. When you've said a little too much, definitely hush. When you hear yourself start to tear down another woman, hush. When everything that comes out of your mouth begins to sound ugly and negative, hush. If you feel like whining, consider whether you'd rather just hush. When you start dredging up empty words to fill the space, it might do well just to hush a moment. Shhhhh. Hear the awesome power of saying nothing at all.

Hussssssshhhhh.

Idle

Lower your internal engine until it's a barely perceptible hum. Idle away an hour watching a robin feed her young. Idle away a day watching the sun move across the sky. Give time over to doing nothing at all. Walk into the forest with no book, no tapes, no paper and pencil, no desire to identify wildflowers or mushrooms or tracks in the snow. When you have walked far enough, simply be idle. Be *of* the forest, not just in it. Pay no attention to what time it is. The day is long for those who idle. Wherever you choose to be, be there and nowhere else. Resist the urge to rehash yesterday's events or to plan tomorrow's. Simply idle your mind, letting it rest at last. Ask nothing of yourself except to while away the time, idly letting it wash over you moment by moment by precious, peaceful moment.

Ignore

Ignore ignorant minds and ignorant actions.
When half-truths or untruths are cast in your
direction, ignore them. When you receive letters
filled with vituperative trash, tear them up and
throw them into the fire. To repel unwanted and
untoward advances, ignore them. Ignore all
kinds of verbal slings and arrows. Turn away,
turn around, and walk away. Turn the other
cheek. Say *Good-bye*, and then hang up the
phone. Pay no attention to the ravings of jealous
fools. Ignore unfounded slurs on your character
and your reputation. Give them no fuel, and
they will eventually die out. To reject, ignore.
To snuff, ignore. You suffer no ignominy when
you choose to ignore.

Imagine

Imagine things being different. Imagine a little less struggle and a lot more joy. Imagine yourself living every moment out of love instead of fear. Imagine making space each and every day just for you. Imagine peace breaking out all over the world. Imagine loving your body just the way it is. Imagine everyone loving it. Imagine working at something that fills your heart and nourishes your soul and challenges your mind and covers rent and food, too! Imagine that everything you need can be provided. Now imagine that it is. Imagine none of your friends dying of breast cancer. Imagine there *is* a Heaven, and it's right here on Earth. Imagine feeling rested and serene and safe and loved each and every day.

Imagine that!

Improvise

Throw away your recipes, your sheet music, your books filled with step-by-step instructions on how to do this and how not to do that. Use cornmeal instead of flour for a different kind of muffin. Bury the cookie cutters. Change the tempo of the concerto when you feel moved to do so. Substitute mocha for bittersweet, almond for vanilla, teal for celadon. Read every decorating magazine you can get your hands on, then toss them away and put the throw pillows on the floor, the rug on the wall, and the library lamp in the downstairs loo. Put a little more of you and a little less of them in everything you do. So what if it's different? Or better? Or worse? If you hate it, start over. Create your own traditions, just like your great-grandparents did. Develop your own personal style—and let Madonna, Di, and all the rest eat their hearts out.

Include

Bring everyone into the circle.

Include the women you've always known and the women you've wanted to meet for a long time. Include the Vietnamese women from down the block. Include the straight women; include the lesbians. Definitely include the women in wheelchairs. Include the Pagans, the Christians, the Catholics, the Buddhists, the Mormons. Include everyone who wants to be included. Include your mother and her friends, your grandmother and her friends. Include your mother-in-law, even if you're divorced. Include the woman who makes $125,000 per year; include the woman on public assistance. Include the brown women, the black women, the white women, the red women. Include the woman with the birthmark covering half her face. Include everyone, and you'll be included, too.

Inherit

Inherit your grandmother's twinkling eyes, her recipe for blintzes. Inherit your father's laugh, his whistle, his strong yet gentle way. Inherit your mother's legs, the dancer's legs. Inherit her willingness to stand up for what's right, her courage to speak out when no one else will. Inherit Aunt Madge's poker face, Nana's unfailing tenacity, your Uncle Willie's half-sister's faith and devotion. Inherit everybody's stories, a couple of skeletons, and who knows how many secrets. Inherit the family smile, that unmistakable nose, the freckles and the dimples, and oh, that hair! Inherit the wind. Inherit the legacy. Inherit the pile of old pictures and protect them until someone, someday, inherits them from you.

Innovate

Do it new, do it different. Do it like nobody's ever done it before. Come up with a new way that's smarter, faster, easier, cheaper. Develop a new style of management. Discover a better way to peel potatoes. Create a whole new model for bringing about social change. Innovate at the office, innovate at the legislature, innovate on the golf course. (Could you be a little more innovative in the bedroom?) Invent something totally new that will erase pantyhose from the face of the Earth. Introduce an attitude that's utterly original and indescribably fresh. Music, movies, tables, computers, houses, makeup, cars. Put things together in a way that's new and unique, and the world will beat a path to your door. While you're at it, could you do something new with the door?

Insist

When you must, insist. Insist that you be given the opportunity to speak. Insist that everyone be given the same. Insist that they listen. Insist that every viewpoint be given credence—no matter who presents it. Insist on the truth; insist that people be willing to dig for it. Insist that the people around you be civil and respectful of all beings. Insist that they stop already with the jokes that aren't funny and the compliments that compliment no one. Insist on a square deal. Insist that people look at you when they talk to you. Insist on nothing less from yourself. When polite isn't quite enough and demanding seems over the top, simply, firmly, clearly insist.

Inspire

Do something very courageous, very bold, very exhilarating, and pass the energy along. Be infectious. Lower your voice and lean in to tell how awesome it is to move halfway across the country with no money, no job, no place to live. Breathe in, breathe out, breathe into another. Tell another woman how you left a suffocating job— so she knows she can do it. Tell a young girl about the thrill of traveling around the world alone—so she knows she can try it. Be as healthy, as vibrant, as beautiful, as authentic as you possibly can be, in a way that speaks silently to others, *You can be this, too.* Smile at other women's dreams and their hopes, and reassure them that they'll survive whatever black hole they're currently navigating. At the beach, tell the young mother of four that you and your ex-husband can talk together, laugh together. Don't just *tell* her that she can be there, too, *show* her. Let her see it in your eyes and hear it in your voice and then breathe it in—*inspire*—herself.

Interrupt

Interrupt injustice and indignities. When someone starts spouting hatred, interrupt her and let her know it's not okay with you. Whether in public or in private, when someone starts dissing people on account of their skin or their clothes or their religion or their finances, interrupt him and tell him you will not continue this conversation. When the meeting has disintegrated into petty infighting and rampant displays of ego, interrupt and insist that participants get back on track. If a woman appears flustered by a man's attentions, interrupt and ask her if she would like to sit with you. A good girl may never interrupt, but a righteous woman always will.

Intuit

Rely on your sixth sense and bypass your brain altogether. If it feels like a good idea, it probably is. If your internal danger signs start flashing and blinking, it probably isn't. Trust your intuition. Honor your gut instinct—that inkling that rises up from your belly and tugs and tugs at you until you finally pay attention. If your intuition tells you not to get on the plane, don't. If that inner voice tells you to walk away from a person or a situation, do. Rely on your intuition and it will serve you well. Intuit the answer; intuit the way out. Intuit the solution to problems large or small. Cultivate your intuition. Believe in it as the reliable and accurate tool it is—and ignore anyone who believes it to be anything else. I can't exactly explain why, but something tells me you can get *intuit*. How does that feel to you?

Invite

Invite almost everyone to nearly everything.
Invite three women on a weekend getaway without even knowing where you're going. Invite
your pigpen roommate to move, and invite
yourself to help her pack. Invite someone from
the office home for dinner. If that person
declines, invite someone else. If you like the way
she moves, invite her to dance. Ditto for him.
Invite yourself to spend an entire Sunday doing
whatever you want. Accept your invitation without reservations. If you want to invite somebody
for a drink, go ahead and do it. Even if the
neighbors will talk. *Especially* if the neighbors
will talk. Invite someone over to play Scrabble,
to make pesto, to read French poetry, to refinish
your floors. Invite whomever you want to your
wedding—and invite absolutely no one you
don't want! If someone shows up at your door
uninvited, remember that you always have the
right, the power, and the privilege to invite that
person to leave.

Jazz

Climb out of the doldrums and jazz things up! Jazz up your personal style. Be brighter, be bolder, bedeck yourself with skirts that swing, with suits that shimmer, with shoes that shine. Jazz up your home. String cows that light up around your doorway. Burn candles, burn incense, burn sage. Burn the midnight oil while you listen to all-time jazz greats. Jazz up the way you think about things. Spend more time in conversation, less time comatose in front of the tube. Read jazzier 'zines; hit jazzier Web sites. Jazz up your cooking with peppers that sting, spices that zing, sauces that sing. If your nights are drab, jazz 'em up. If you're too jazzed, cool it down. Make it mellow, make it swing, make it anything and everything.

Just be sure you make it jazz!

Join

Join hands, join hearts. Join up with other women who think the same way you do. Join up with others who don't. Join only organizations that are committed to real change and real issues and a true vision. Join a chorus and sing. Join a book group and read and think and discuss. Join a neighborhood association and plant gardens or lobby for parking or lobby against the twenty-four-hour superstore down the street. Join others who are taking a personal stand against intolerance. Join a cooperative anything. Join people who get together and dance and chant and pray and meditate and give thanks. Join your local hospice organization and help bring dignity to the dying. Join your friends at a coffeehouse and ponder the meaning of friendship. Even if you're a nonjoiner, it's never too late to join the human race.

Journey

Journey your way through life. Experience
the adventure and forget about the destination (whatever *that* is!). Journey across the
world to a place that looks, smells, tastes,
and feels different from any place you've ever
been. Journey to your family's homeland.
Journey to humanity's homeland. Journey on
a bicycle, on a train, on a ship, on foot. Journey through the pages of a book. Chant and
drum and meditate your way into a journey
of the soul. Journey without a map and
make one up as you go. Journey more deeply
inside than ever before. Journey in your
wheelchair. Journey alone or with others.
Never journey in a hurry (it's not a journey
then, it's a road trip). Journey without a
camera. Instead, imprint every image directly
onto the cells of your body. Journey empty
and you are sure to return full.

Jump

Jump for joy, jump into the fray, jump high enough to touch the sky. Jump farther, faster. Jump in time to the music. First, make the music. Jump steady. Close your eyes and jump. Jump into the pit of your own despair and stay there until you figure the way out. Jump into a pool when it's eighty-six degrees. Jump into a lake when it's forty-nine degrees. Jump over obstacles, jump into your shoes every morning and out of them each night. Jump over a fence in your stocking feet. Jump out of the way of danger when you feel it coming. When someone barks *Jump!,* don't. (Did I mention jump for joy?)

Keep

Keep a sweet and lovely secret for twenty-seven years. Keep a little something from someone who has passed over. Keep your hair out of your eyes—at least when you're trying to read. Remember your Sabbath and keep it holy. When you're feeling vulnerable, keep to yourself and keep others at arm's length. Keep the faith, no matter what. Keep hope alive in the face of unspeakable pain. Keep moving and growing. Keep reminding yourself that it's the journey and not the destination that counts. Keep your body healthy—it's the only one you get this time around. Keep a little bit of candy for yourself, even if you have to keep it way in the back of the freezer. Keep it for a rainy day. Keep hoping for rain. Keep yourself grounded and centered in the midst of chaos—and always keep an eye out for those who don't.

Kick

When you've got mountains to climb, kick yourself into high gear. Kick into overdrive. Kick yourself in the pants and kick up a little dust. Playing soccer? Kick low. Jumping hurdles? Kick high. Kick proverbial butt. When they push your buttons, kick up a fuss. Go kicking and screaming. Kick the habit. Kick all of them. Kick the can, kick the bucket. Never kick the dog. Pretend you're a Radio City Music Hall Rockette and kick the ceiling. Kick up your heels and have a ball. Then kick yourself for not doing it more often. Sit in a coffee shop and kick back. Kick around lofty ideas until they kick you out at closing time.

Kiss

Plant a peck on the cheek of a child. Kiss the hand of a crone. Brush your lips against a river-worn stone, against the back of your own left hand. Press up against the lips of your sweetheart and mingle your tongues and your souls. In the ecstasy of it all, don't forget to breathe. Share sloppy, wet dog kisses. Kiss your iguana. Kiss in public and pretend no one is looking, even though you know they all are. Kiss in the doctor's waiting room and in the art gallery and in the walk-in freezer. Kiss where you think no one has kissed before. Blow a kiss good-bye from an ocean liner or at the train station and watch it fly through the air and land on its intended target. Kiss a frog without even thinking about a handsome prince.

Kiss the moon goodnight when it's full,

and feel her kiss you back.

Knead

Unplug your electric bread machine and do
it the old-fashioned way. Work bubbling,
breathing life into flour and water and yeast.
Push down and away, now turn and fold,
now again and again. Knead sourdough
bread dough and pizza dough and dough for
cinnamon rolls and crescent rolls and pret-
zels. Knead alongside women in dirt-floored
huts, in inner-city kitchens, in camp, in
architecturally correct spaces that need for
nothing. Work with clay, knead the life into
it. Knead the knots out of someone's shoulders. Work them out and stretch them out
and knead them out. Knead your foot when
it cramps up. Build a rhythm. Go deeper.
Now push down and away, now turn and
fold, now again. With your knees, with your
knuckles, now knead.

Knit

Knit by the fire in the autumn of the year. Knit
all winter long, woolen socks and mittens, hats
and leggings. Knit a magical scarf that tells magical stories, mystical yarns. Knit ten thousand
stitches and, at every stitch, recite a prayer. Knit
with wool, cotton, handspun yarns, curlicued
and mohair-soft and fuzzy. Knit, purl, knit, purl.
Knit a family together. Knit a community
together, drawing each thread closer and linking
with the others. Knit a row, purl a row, knit a
row, purl a row. Knit for the baby not yet born a
hooded shawl, tiny feet warmers, a blanket dyed
with the marigold's gold. Knit with your great-
aunt's needles, smooth wood or ivory, the mouths
of whales, clicking softly, softly. Knit and purl,
and knit and purl, and knit and purl, and knit.

Know

Know nothing, know everything. Know without asking. Know before the phone rings because you feel it in your gut. Know what the ancient women knew because you feel it in your bones. Don't always let on that you know. Learn about the phases of the moon, and then you'll know. Learn to write from Brenda Ueland, and then you'll know. Know that what you feel is real. Know yourself, your strengths and your lesser strengths. Know how to turn off the main gas line if you have to. Know at least three constellations in the night sky. Know the way home even if you didn't drive. Know when to leave and when to stay. Know, really know, how beautiful you are. Know as many words as you can remember —and make up the rest. Don't always assume that he knows more. Know that now is all that matters, and know how to be here now.

Kvetch

Once or twice.

Three times at the most.

Then quit your complaining, and get over it.

It might make you feel well, but the rest of us
are sick and tired of hearing it!

Labor

Labor hard to bring forth your creations.
Labor long into the night. Feel your body
as a sacred vessel, pouring out the fruits
of your labors. Give birth to an idea, a
vision you've carried for decades. Sweat
and grunt and moan low to bring forward your music, your words, your
dance, your dream. Yourself. Feel yourself
ready to open. Hear yourself cry out from
the pain. Scream for everyone to leave
you alone. Beg for everyone to hold you
close. Surround yourself with women
while you labor. Ask them to hold your
hands, to rub your back, to bring you
warm blankets and cool drinks and an
extra box of diskettes. Know that whatever you birth, when the labor is over, the
hard work begins.

Laugh

Laugh when it all becomes so ludicrous there's nothing else to do. Laugh big, deep laughs that open up your throat and your lungs and your belly. Laugh alone, laugh in concert with other laughers. At the movies, laugh when no one else laughs—and let them wonder what they've missed. Laugh at your own mistakes, your own foibles, your own foolishness. Laugh in the face of fear. Laugh until you cry, laugh until you have a stomachache. Let laughter be your medicine, your companion, your music of joy from within. Laugh in school or at work or in church. Get up and leave the room if you must. Laugh in public. Bend over laughing, fall to the ground laughing, roll on the floor laughing. Start an entire room laughing, start the whole world laughing. And don't stop until you have the last laugh. She who laughs, lives.

Lead

If you were born to be a leader, lead! Take
the lead if it isn't given to you first. Blaze the
trail. Usher in a new era. Lead your people,
lead your generation, lead us all into the
promise of a new tomorrow. When the people lead, the leaders will follow. Take the lead
position and give others a target to aim for.
Lead the way to victory; lead the way to freedom. If it has always been hard for you to
follow, now it's time for you to lead. Take
one woman by the hand and lead her to a life
of peace. Lead her back to herself. If all the
world's a stage, we need our leading ladies.
And that means we need you now, more than
ever, to lead.

Leap

Close your eyes and step out over the edge.
Leave behind the baggage that will weigh
you down. Stretch farther than you
believed you could. Gather your courage;
you'll need it. Let go of every one of those
twenty-seven reasons why you can't do it.
Drop the concepts of failure, of success.
Just do it. Know that you'll fly or you
won't. The ground isn't that far away—and
if you create a safety net before you go,
someone will somehow break your fall.
Maybe falling is okay. You're not jumping
off Mt. Kilimanjaro; you're simply testing
your reach, bridging what seemed to be an
impossible chasm. Sell off your furniture
and take a trip. Cut up your credit cards.
Become houseless for a while. Ask the children's father to take them for a month
while you write or train or sing or sleep.
Ask again. Move far away. Leap.

Learn

Live to learn. This year, learn more than you learned last year. Learn something totally different. To learn more about yourself, learn more about other women. Learn how things work and how to fix them when they don't. Learn to fend for yourself, to hold your own when under attack. Learn to write with your nondominant hand; learn to draw from the right side of your brain. Learn to ski, to play cribbage, to carve, to speak Russian, to cook Oriental, to dance Swedish folk dances. Learn something you never knew about your great-grandmother. As soon as you learn something, start teaching it to someone else. Learn for the sake of learning. Learn because you love to learn.

Leave

If you must, leave. Leave for your own safety or that of your children. Leave under cover of darkness if that's the only way. Leave when you feel so suffocated you can hardly breathe. Leave because your very soul will wither and die if you stay. Leave before it's too late, but not too early. Know that if you leave, you may not have the choice of going back. Leave a trace of yourself everywhere you go. Leave them laughing. Leave them crying. Always, always, leave them wanting more. For a change, be the first to leave—or the last. Don't leave in the morning without saying good-bye. Leave your shoes outside the door and leave early enough to get there on time. Don't forget to leave a note!

Let

Let it be. Just let it be and let go. Let her have her way, then let go of it once and for all. Let her have her way, then let a sleeping dog lie. Let it be okay. Let it be. Let there be peace on Earth, and let it begin with you. Let up on the gas and let your mind wander. Let yourself go. Let your hair down; let it swing free and easy. Let yourself have a break now and then, will you? Let yourself live again and love again. If someone has let you down, let it pass. Let bygones be bygones. Let the truth be known, now and forever. Let the bells ring and the chimes chime. When someone lets you in on a little secret, don't let on that you already know.

Lick

Eat shrimp, rice, salad, pudding, watermelon
with your fingers, and then lick them clean.
Thoroughly enjoy yourself, especially if it leaves
others aghast. Lick the salt off your lover's sweaty
body. Better yet, lick it off your own. At least
once in your life, let a dog lick your face. (Actually, once may be enough.) Lick your ice-cream
cone as provocatively as you want no matter
who's watching. Get a big lollipop with swirls
of different colors and lick it for old times' sake.
(Stop the lick before you get sick.) Lick your
wounds in private, skulking off to your cave or
den like a wild animal. When you cut your finger, lick your own blood. If you can't join 'em,
lick 'em! Lick your lips if they're dry or for no
reason whatsoever. Lick the bowl clean of every
last bit of chocolate icing. Lick anything that
comes to mind. Yes, anything.

Lighten

Oh, lighten up. Why must everything always be so heavy? So what if you broke your finger and your hard drive crashed and your deadline is in nine days? Lighten up! What does it really matter if the baby threw up on your good silk suit and the big meeting is at ten o'clock and everything else is at the cleaner's? Just lighten up; it's not the end of the world. So what if you came home from a three-week vacation and there were only three messages on your machine—all from bill collectors? What's the big deal if the cat left hairballs on the nine-layer cake for your great-grandmother's ninety-fifth birthday party? Is it really so terrible that you spent four years crocheting an afghan and then your partner accidentally put it in with the hot-water load?

Will you please just lighten up???

Like

Like yourself just the way you are. Like the way you look, like the way you talk. Like the way you get things done. Like your hair, most of the time. Like your breasts, whatever they are or are not. Like that chipped front tooth. Like the fact that there isn't anybody, anywhere, exactly like you. Like your job. Like the way it's sort of like having a family. Like your boss, and especially like it when she likes you. Like the driver who delivers the overnight mail—a lot. Like the way you've done up your apartment. Like the way you've stenciled your home office. Like the music the people play next door. Like being thirty-three, like being forty, like being sixty-five. (Remember what it was like to be thirteen!) Like the way your friends show you how much they like you. Like how it feels when you like them right back.

Linger

Stop rushing. Just stop. Sip the last drops of your tea instead of gulping them. Finish your conversation before running to the next item on your calendar. Pause and watch the woman who sings opera on the street, the woman who stir-fries the Chinese food, the young girl playing the violin as though she was born with it in her hand. Look at the sky for just a bit longer before you get into your car. Pick a leaf of mint or sage; before continuing on, rub it between your fingers and smell how delicious it smells. Look into someone's eyes just a bit longer than you thought you could. Linger over coffee, linger at the newsstand, linger over lunch. Linger longer in bed, in the park, on the river. Of course, linger longer at love.

Listen

Sit in silence and see how much there is to hear. **Listen to people.** What are they really saying? What are they not saying? Listen to the very last notes of every song. **Listen to a sunset;** listen to the sounds on your street well after midnight. Listen to your intuition, to your own inner voice—the one you can hear only when the din of every day is diminished. **Hear the rustle of a leaf,** the call of a bullfrog, the pop and crackle from your wood stove. Savor the call of a gentle breeze, the flap of a bird's wings, the fanfare of a summer thunderstorm. Listen with your toes, listen with your heart, and always, *always* **listen to that which is never spoken.**

Live

As long as you're alive, why not live? Live
life to the fullest. Live it up. Live in the
moment. Live as though you had only
twenty-four hours to live. Live the life
you've always wanted. Live for yourself—
not for others, alive or dead. Live on the
edge a bit; it's the only place from which
you can take a leap. Live the life that is
yours alone. Live wherever you want, with
whomever you want, however you want,
but live! Don't just get a life—create one.
Don't just step into someone else's life—
design your own. Don't confuse real life
with what you see on TV or at the movies.
Live free or die (even if you're not from
New Hampshire). Live so that when you're
dead, people will remark less on what you
did in life—and more on how you lived.

Look

Look at yourself, how beautiful you are. Look at the love that pours from your eyes, look at how your wisdom and experience are written all over your face. Look at the beauty of other women. All of them. Look at their lips, full and ripe, thin and dry. Look at their skin, smooth and wrinkled, creamy and coarse, olive and terra-cotta and peach and ebony and freckled and scarred. Look at how women move. See them stride, see them shuffle, see them with eyes on the ground and eyes on the sky. See them inch slowly like the turtle; see them fly like the eagle. Look at the muscles in a woman's body; look at the serenity in a blind woman's face; look at the rugged hands of a laborer. Look at every person you meet with compassion and love. Look for the good in their hearts and you're sure to stumble on the good in your own.

Love

Love freely, love deeply,
love purely. Love yourself the way you've
always wanted to be loved, and love others the same way. Love
well, love often. Find it in your heart to love those who have never
shown you love—for they need it most of all. Give so much love that
you're certain to get some back. Open your heart to the woman who
lives on the sidewalk with her two daughters. Love her. Have
compassion for the man who fired you from the job you loved
most of all. Love him. Love all the Earth has to offer—her
people, her birds, her stones, insects, trees, mice, and
oceans. Love something—anything!—with a
passion. Love something larger than yourself.
Call it Goddess, call it God, call it
Nature, call it the Divine, call it
Source, call it Betty.
Call it Love.

Lunch

Lunch on soup and salad. Lunch on cakes and wine. Lunch on food whose first name isn't *fast*. Lunch on leftovers: last night's spaghetti, that last half an eggroll, the last piece of pie. Lunch business, lunch birthdays, lunch because you need the break. No matter the weather, get out for lunch. Lunch crunchy, lunch smooth, lunch sandwich. Lunch on a tablecloth, lunch on a picnic blanket, lunch on a stool at the luncheonette. Lunch deli, lunch street food, lunch lavish. Lunch quick. Lunch long. Lunch right up until dinner. Lunch alone while you study. Lunch with a friend you haven't seen for years. Lunch with your lover. Love lunch. Have a blind lunch, have a silent lunch. If there's no time to eat, then laugh lunch.

Make

Make every day count. Make love more often and more sweetly. Make that phone call you've put off for months. Make it short and to the point, but make it now. Make something with your hands. Use sticks and yarn and macaroni and old ribbon and bits of things that you find here and there. Make it unlike anything you've ever made before or will ever make again. Make homemade peach jam. Okay, make strawberry. Make changes. Make as much money as you want, and give away every penny you don't really need. After a misunderstanding—or an out-and-out argument—make up quickly, before it's too late. Make magic. Make a silk purse out of a sow's ear and defy anyone who says you can't. Make a fresh start. Make your house your own. Make your life your own. Make up a wild and fanciful tale about yourself, then make up your mind whether to make it known to anyone's ears but your own.

Market

Stop by the corner market, the outdoor market with tables piled high, the co-op market, the grocery. Pick up a few things for dinner, for the weekend. Gently fondle the fruits, soft and ripened mangoes, sweet slices of melon, pears tender to the touch, apples, oranges, kiwi, strange and exotic fruits with unfamiliar names. Ogle the avocados, eyeball the eggplant, sniff the cilantro, the basil, the fennel. Fill your basket, your canvas bag, string tote, backpack, with bagels lying down and baguettes standing up. Onion, potatoes, and carrots on the bottom, lettuce on the top, a box of pasta, two tomatoes, six eggs, and a lemon. A spring bouquet peeks over the top, next to the candy bar you'll eat on the way home from the market. Tomorrow you'll market again.

Massage

Touch another body with your hands. Warm
your palms first. Add a bit of lotion or oil. Feel
the pulse of life under your fingertips. Don't be
afraid to use your knuckles, your fists, your feet.
Roll a muscle between your fingers. Find that
place where sheer pleasure moves up toward a
hint of discomfort. Listen to another body. Back
off if you need to. Massage your mother's feet
lovingly. Massage a baby's leg gently. Massage an
animal's neck, the scalp of someone's great-
grandmother, hands that are sore from piano
keyboards or computer keyboards or from holding on too tightly for too long. Massage necks
and shoulders and lower backs everywhere.
Don't think about sex. Okay, think about it.
But really, just massage.

Meander

The shortest distance between two points may not always be the richest. Take a detour from the straight and narrow. Meander down roads you never traveled before. Meander slowly, go in circles, bump into dead ends, turn around, start again, crawl into caves dripping with moisture. This time, try the path that seems to go nowhere and see where you end up. Meander. Meander along the way from problem to solution, to resolution. Try this way, now that, now another. Follow the bends and twists and tunnels along your path. Traverse the peaks and valleys. Remember that there are no detours, no wrong turns. Wherever you meander, you are well on your way.

Meet

Meet at the cafe, at the library, at the produce
section of the market, behind the train station,
under the old stone bridge. Meet at noon, at first
light, at four-thirty-six, when the moon is full,
when everyone else in the house is fast asleep.
Meet for no reason at all except to meet. Meet to
talk or to listen. Meet so you can hold hands and
bounce up and down and yell together. Meet in
silence. Meet secretly. Meet another person
halfway. Meet your heart's desire in a most
unlikely place. Try for a meeting of the hearts—
then a meeting of the minds. Take steps to meet a
new person every third day. When you're forty-
five, look in the mirror and meet your mother in
a whole new way. Kneel down to meet a child.
Lean in to meet a willing pair of lips.

Meet on *your* terms,
    and meet yourself in the process.

Mend

When things are frayed and torn, mend them. Mend yourself when you've come apart at the seams. Put your pieces back together with a steady, patient stitch. Sit down in a comfy chair with that basket of clothes and mend them. Bring out your threads and needles and buttons. Listen to Lena Horne while you mend. Put the pieces back together. Mend a relationship that stretched until it couldn't stretch anymore. Mend your broken heart. Piece together all the beautiful squares and circles and diamonds that you are. Find how your mothering self and your child self, your business self and your artistic self can all fit together in a colorful, integrated whole. Like a patchwork quilt. Mend that ancient rift in your family. Make amends. Mend that hole where you let parts of yourself be sucked away time and time again. Amend your agreements with people as you change and as they change. Before you reach an end, take time to mend.

Mentor

Take another woman under your wing and help her learn to fly. Share what you know—and how you learned it. Show her whom to watch out for—and precisely why. Lead her through an initiation, and guide her through the pitfalls you've already survived. Tell her what she'll never read in the manual. Maybe she's younger than you, maybe she's not. Maybe she reminds you of you, maybe she doesn't. Maybe she's your daughter. Mentor her through high school, through college, through her Ph.D. Mentor her into business, into government, into the theater. Stay close enough to hold her gently by the arm if she needs it—and far enough away to give her room to fall if she must. Tell her you believe in her and you want to see her soar. Watch her eyes become big and wide— and wonder why they call it *men*tor, anyway.

Mind

Yes I do mind, and thank you for asking. I mind if you smoke; I mind if you take that seat next to me. I mind that you're trying to strike up a stupid conversation when I'm obviously enjoying my solitude. I mind it when you ignore the women in the room. I mind that a man doing the same job as I do is paid more. I especially mind because I'm doing it better. I mind that there's always a long line outside the women's room at intermission. I mind that most of the women in most of the movies take off most of their clothes, and I mind that the men don't. I mind that I pay more at the dry cleaner's—and my friends mind, too. Mind if I say one more thing? I mind when you think I'm a nag when I mind. On second thought, I don't mind if you do. . . .

Mingle

Come out of your shell and mingle. Stroll the downtown mall, sit on the grass outside the courthouse, stand in groups of two or three waiting for the cinema to open. Sit next to people you don't know in tiny bakeries and crowded espresso bars. Mingle and converse and share a table and the newspaper and the honey bear. Smile and ask a simple question. Strike up a conversation. Go to a reception and mingle in a sea of new faces. After the lecture, mingle with the others who admire the author as much as you do. Mingle with the others who left early and are mingling by the magazines. When a knocked-out transformer takes your TV and your computer and your air conditioner, go outside and mingle with your neighbors in the dark. Mingle and meet and talk and remember how pleasant it is just to mingle.

Move

Your address, your body, your bookshelf. Shake out anything in your life that's rusty, stiff, or stuck and get it into motion. Take a walk, take a hike, take a step away from stagnating jobs, relationships, and life patterns. Change perspective. Move closer to people who meet you with authenticity and who nourish your wildest dreams. Move away from everybody else. You don't have to move mountains; shifting a single pebble can work wonders. Make your move—*any move*—now. If you wait until you have more money, more security, more grace, more anything, you'll never move anywhere at all.

Muse

Lose yourself in dreamy days. Close your eyes and turn off the rooftop chatter and let your thoughts wander with the ease of a feather floating on a warm summer breeze. Wonder as you wander. Muse away the afternoon awash in fantasy. Go in and out of this and that and nothing in particular. Follow a bumblebee into the heart of a blossom and see where it takes you. Imagine your own trip to Wonderland, your journey to the deepest center of Inner Earth, your flight on angel wings. Climb onto the soft and silky back of a unicorn and be carried far away to that unknown place where rainbows live between the rains. Call your muses to your side. Let them hold your hands and whisper words in your ears and breathe into your being the sweet, holy breath of inspiration.

Name

Name three women who have made a difference in your life. Ask someone to name a school after one of them, or a park, or any sacred space where women are very much welcome. Name your daughter after a goddess—and be sure she knows for whom she was named. Name her after a vegetarian burger, after your favorite feminist restaurant, after anything proud and strong and beautiful. Name yourself in a special ceremony of your own creation. Name yourself after your great-great-grandmother who played the saxophone, after a flower whose rare beauty takes your breath away, after an enchanted place you read about on a hot summer day when your hair was in pigtails. Name your car Iphelia, name your bed Tatiana. Discover a sweet and lovely spot in the woods and give it a secret name that only you know. When the moon is full and you feel especially dazzling, name yourself Lunesca for the night.

Nap

Whenever you want to, whenever you need to. Curl up like a Siamese cat in the sun and snooze. Nap after lovemaking, nap after shopping, nap after finally, finally having that conversation with your neighbor that you put off for so long. Nap on the sofa on a rainy Sunday. Nap in the bath. Let the regenerative power of sleep take you. Let the phone ring. Let them all wonder why your office door is closed. You're in the sweet, sweet arms of Morpheus, and the quarterly reports can just wait a few minutes more. Spread out a towel in the grass, on the floor of the airport, on sand anywhere you find it. Don't explain, don't rationalize, don't justify.

Just nap.

Need

Need other people without being ashamed of it. Need help with the mortgage, with the kids, with the car, with the plumbing, with getting it all done every single day. Without feeling guilty for needing. Allow yourself to be needful without being needy. Acknowledge that you need more love, more friends, more support, more freedom to be your authentic self. Let others need you. Go out and get what you need, and know that it's okay. Know the difference between what you want and what you need. Need peace, need to weep, need to be held, and don't apologize. Need to dance, need to achieve, need to soar, need to risk, need to be alone. When you feel like you need everything, you may need to accept that's just what you need.

Nest

Create a home that's as safe and soothing and comforting as you can make it. Let order or chaos rule as you dictate. Fold your towel in perfect form—or toss it into the corner with abandon. Surround yourself with true treasures you've found along the way: a perfect pebble, a near-perfect bowl, the pocket watch that stopped working after your friend's mother died. Soften corners with sheets and fabric and pillows; soften the sounds of traffic with curtains and wind chimes at the window and bells hung from door-jambs. Feather a nest that will weather your most violent emotional storms and will remain intact while the world thrashes and shakes around you. Know that you can shut your windows and doors to the world, and sink into your "egg place" when you need to recharge, refresh, rebirth yourself into fresh, new ways of living and being.

Nibble

Bite, bite, chew, chew, nibble.
Nibble at that piece of cake in the freezer
until you've nibbled it into oblivion. When
you're faced with a daunting assignment or a
killer project, nibble away at it in small,
manageable pieces. Nibble your way
through an 850-page novel. When a lot of
people are trying to shove a lot of things
down your throat, don't swallow until you
chew on them for a while. Pick it all apart
so you can digest it better. Bite, bite, chew,
chew, nibble. Set a long-term goal and then
nibble at it bit by bit over time. Don't bite
off more than you can chew. If you can't
consume the whole thing at once, don't try.
Don't gulp, don't gobble; just nibble. Bite,
bite, chew, chew, nibble.

Nourish

Feed yourself whatever makes you feel strong and satisfied inside and out. Know the difference between nourishing your hunger and feeding your stomach. Nourish yourself with a bowl of homemade soup, a cherry pie, a mason jar of black-eyed Susans next to the bed, an hour at the library, two hours of absolutely nothing. Nourish your soul, your heart, your spirit. When you wake up, nourish yourself with a walk, a meditation, a prayer, a conversation with a friend. Midday, satisfy your craving for exercise, for music, for writing, for solitude, for companionship. Snack on a book, some time out for your sewing, a cup of tea and two shortbread biscuits. Round out every day with the essential nourishment categories: peace, love, quiet, and creativity.

Nurture

Nurture yourself. First, always, yourself. Yes! Give yourself the time, the love, the undivided attention you so often give to others. Sing, dance, read, cook, sew, run, swim, be. Then you can nurture the rest of the world—but not until. Then have babies, create beauty, plant gardens, build a home, teach a child, mother a puppy, heal the wounded, guide a community or a nation or a planet. It doesn't matter what it is. Give from your purest heart and demand nothing in return. Nurture with unconditional love, with time, with money, with wisdom. Help something—anything—to grow. But first, nurture yourself. First, always, yourself. Some will call you selfish, but you'll know that self-care is the first step. The first step in learning to nurture.

Observe

Stop, drop to your knees, and just watch. Don't try to figure out why or how a bee drinks sweet nectar from a lilac. Just observe. See those two people in line? Watch their body language. Don't stare, just observe. Watch with the keen eyes of a stalking feline. Keep watching, and see the invisible. See the shadow of a gesture. See the smile that no one else sees. Observe who walks her talk, and who only talks it. Observe a dancer who's on stage and another who isn't. Watch a swan move across a lake. Observe how effortless it seems—and remember that she's swimming like crazy just below the surface. Observe your own way of moving through life. Do others observe you gliding effortlessly—or thrashing about above the surface? Witness the flare of your own emotions, the flash of your own passion. Watch yourself watching yourself. Then watch what happens when you don't.

Offer

Make an offering before you're asked. Offer something that money can't buy. Offer to baby-sit so a harried new mother can take a break. Offer to take blankets to the homeless. Offer to sit with someone who's dying—or to sit with someone who's been sitting with someone who's dying. Offer to wash her hair, massage her feet. Make an offering that can't be refused. Offer half your food to someone who's hungrier than you are. Offer to lend your laptop or your car or your lawn chairs or anything you're not really using every minute of every day. Offer what you have to give. Offer a tiny bit of yourself. Then offer a larger part. Never offer what you can't give. Offer yourself the gift of offering to others. After your offer has been received, move on, and offer again.

Open

Open your mouth, exhale, and say *Ahhhhhhh*.
Do whatever you can to open your heart. Now
open it wider. Open yourself to deeper levels of
feeling. Open your eyes and take a good look
around you. Open every one of your chakras
and let the energy of life move through you. (If
you don't know what chakras are, open yourself
to finding out.) Open up all the places inside
you that have shut down and rusted over the
years. Open the gate to your secret garden.
Open that tattered box in the attic and touch
everything inside. Open that envelope one more
time. Open a book that has always seemed too
intense, and read it. Open a jar of cashew butter, and eat it with your fingers. When opportunity knocks, open the door. When you want to
breathe, open your mouth and open your lungs.
Open up yourself and see how easy it becomes
to open up to others. Now open wide. . . .

Overdo

Don't just push your envelope, rip right through it! Stay up too late and dance too vigorously and carouse over the top. The next day, sleep too late and do too little. Eat too much, too rich. Spend too much money. Write too many checks. Buy more CDs than you need, then give too many away. Watch four videos in a row, take them all back, and get three more. Play computer games all afternoon. Break for two bags of popcorn and a six-pack of diet something, then go back and play some more. Soak in the tub until your fingers and toes are totally pruned. Go in for just a trim, and get a perm. Get some highlights. Get waxed. Once in a while, give yourself everything you want—and then some. And then some more. Just don't overdo it, okay?

Own

Own all that is yours and nothing else. Own your own weaknesses, your own fears, your own wounds. Insist that others own theirs. Own up to your own mistakes. Be your own woman, beholden to no one. Own your life, lock, stock, and barrel. Speak your own mind, sing your own song. Own your own truth and your own power without stepping on anyone else's. Own only as many things as you need and no more. Be careful not to let your possessions own you. Consider owning less: it's not what you own, it's what you have access to. The less you own, the less they can take away. Never try to own other people, no matter how much you believe you love them. Walk your own walk, talk your own talk, and waste no time moving away from anyone who believes that you can be owned.

Paint

Pick up a brush. Dip it in water and glide a watery blue across a sheet of paper. Pick up a brush. Coat every bristle with a smooth white, a fiery red, a verdant green, and lay smooth, broad strokes on clean-to-the-bone wood. Paint your lips if it makes you want to smile more often. Paint your toes, your fingers, your cheeks, your wrists, your ears, and your nose if it makes you want to dance more. Paint the pictures that are your life. Paint four T-shirts, five smooth stones from the bed of a creek. Paint every wall in your bedroom a different color. Then paint them again. Paint daisies on your doorway, circles on your floor, spiders in the hall. Paint with the eye of a child and the soul of a rainbow.

Pamper

Pamper yourself and enjoy every minute. Spend an hour putting your favorite lotion on every bit of skin you can reach. Attend to your every whim. Have a facial, a tarot card reading, a massage, a soak. Believe you deserve it, and enjoy every minute. Make yourself fresh-squeezed juice and serve it to yourself in the most elegant glass you own. Stretch and lie and loll in the sun like a cat. Take all weekend to read the paper. Take a long nap. Take an even longer walk. Eat whatever you want, whenever you want. Cook something elegant and involved just for you, or skip the whole eating thing altogether. Go see a movie in the middle of the day (*and don't you dare feel a bit of guilt!*). Read something trashy. Learn how to treat yourself to indulgences large and small, and if you can't—find somebody who can.

Partner

Hook up with somebody to do something! Find a running partner, a bridge partner, a dance partner, a coin-collecting partner. If your business is getting larger than you can handle, consider getting a business partner. If you're yearning for the companionship and intimacy that partnering brings, go for it. Find a housemate, a roommate, a best friend, a lover. Partner so you have someone to sleep late with, to cook lasagna with, to watch videos with, to drink milkshakes with. Have lots of partners: a going-to-the-symphony-once-a-month partner, a surfing-the-Internet partner, a partner for traveling around to powwows, a let's-have-lunch-and-talk partner. Partner, and you shall be partnered.

Pause

Wait a moment.

Take a breath.

Pause.

Before you react, before you speak. Pause. Before it all comes spilling out, take a breath. Pause. Before you say something you're bound to regret later, pause. When someone says *I love you*, pause before saying *I love you, too*. After you've raced to your two o'clock appointment and raced to find a parking space and raced two blocks in the rain, before you open the door, pause. Breathe out, breathe in, breathe out. Before the discussion escalates into an argument, pause. Before you raise your hand to strike a child, pause long and hard. Punctuate your day with pauses. Collect your thoughts. Pause. Feel the breeze on your face. Pause. Say a prayer. Pause. Take a breath. Pause.

Peel

Start with an onion, and cry all you like.
Take the peel off an apple in one long,
continuous spiral, and let it fall gently to
the floor. Peel an orange slowly, and notice
how each section exposes its softest, juiciest
inner self in turn. See how easily a banana
peels. Peel old wallpaper off a wall and
imagine who put it there in the first place.
Strip the cheap linoleum off your kitchen
floor and see what treasure lies underneath.
Strip away everything you don't really need
in your life and start with a clean slate.
Peel away the layers that keep you from
exposing some of the most tender parts of
yourself. Peel off all that emotional clothing you've been hiding behind. Piece by
piece, layer by layer, slowly, softly, make
your way to the core of who you really are.

Persuade

Do it gently. Don't push, don't argue, don't threaten. Persuade. Persuade with your own unique blend of wisdom, logic, charm, and wiles. Persuade the landlord to come down on the rent. Persuade the town council to approve your permit. Persuade the puppy down the street to give you back what's left of your shoe. When the airline ticket clerk says there are no seats left, persuade him otherwise. When the security guard says

Absolutely not, you may not use the bathroom, persuade her to think again. Don't yell, don't bully. Persuade. Invoke your powers of persuasion. Persuade yourself and you can do it. Can do nearly anything. Do it gently. Don't push, don't argue, don't threaten. Persuade.

Pick

Pick your friends wisely. When you have a few minutes, pick up the living room. Pick up all those magazines, that half-read mail, those stray dishes. When time is running out, pick up your pace. Pick up a pizza for dinner. Pick up Chinese food. Pick up the phone and order. Choose the pick of the litter. (All right, pick the runt out of fear that no one else will pick him.) Pick your own strawberries in the summer; pick your own pumpkins in the fall. In winter, pick your way across the ice. Go back and pick up the pieces. Pick up where you left off. Pick through all the shorts at the rummage sale until you find the pair with the twenty-dollar bill in the pocket. Now go back to the dresses, and pick out the one that nobody else would dare pick.

Picnic

Eat outdoors, where everything tastes better.
Picnic in a park on a high, grassy hill. Spread
out your blanket and your cheeses and crackers,
your olives, smoked fish and terrine, hazelnut
cake, and your thermos of iced mocha lattes.
Picnic in the backyard. Carry out the half-
finished jar of peanut butter, all three of the
near-empty jellies your aunt made, and whatever bread you can find that isn't moldy. Grab a
bag of cookies. Picnic in the city, before your
one-thirty meeting. Open up your attaché and
dig out your low-fat yogurt (vanilla), your
orange (navel), and that spritzer (raspberry)
you never got around to yesterday. Any season,
anywhere, any time, when you can choose
where you want to eat, always pick picnics.

Plant

Put a seed, any seed, in a dark, warm, moist place. Call it a daffodil, call it a tomato, call it a book, call it a baby. Put your seed in an old cracked pot or put it out by the back fence in that spot of earth where the wild violets used to grow. Plant your wishes, your hopes, your dreams in that secret garden that encircles your heart. Take care not to bury them too deeply. Plant your new ideas at work, where there's plenty of fertilizer. Then give your seeds exactly what they need to grow—no more, no less. Be patient and let your seeds flower in their time. You can't reap a harvest if you don't plant.

Plateau

Sometimes the ups and downs of life need to be balanced by the evens. Between your peaks and valleys, plateau. For a while, seek neither the highest heights nor the deepest depths. Let things be on an even keel. Plateau. Give yourself a respite from the drama and the turmoil. Take a break from the incessant push to find a new job, to upgrade your computer, to meet the perfect somebody, to gain ten pounds or to lose twenty, to move to a new city, to go back to school. When things level off, let them stay level. Recharge and refresh your batteries. Look to the horizon without rushing to touch it up close. There will be more highs; there will be more lows. But for now, take it easy: plateau.

Play

Make room in your life for play. Play hopscotch, play checkers, play Frisbee. Play with other women, play with the children in the playground, play with animals. Play with yourself. Sit in a circle and play music. Play the drums, play the piano, play the harmonica, play a metal tin filled with pins and needles and pennies. Just play for the way it makes you feel young and carefree. Play basketball for the first time in a hundred years or so. Laugh and sweat and holler when you play. Play solitaire and cheat a tiny bit if you feel like it. Play simply to play. Play before you work, and see your work become a little more playful. Play quietly indoors on a rainy day. Better yet, go outside and play in the mud. Every day, remember to play.

Pleasure

Discover the delight of pleasuring yourself, of playing your own body like the finely crafted instrument it is. Pleasure yourself on a gray, rainy morning or beside a rock in a meadow covered with wildflowers. Learn the pleasure that comes from pleasuring another. It doesn't have to be sex; it does have to be pleasure. Have chocolate banana cream pie twice a day if that's your pleasure. Find your pleasure in music: sultry jazz or exuberant strings or the low, slow call of a cello. Embrace the pleasure in a job well done, in finishing a race, in completing the simple task they said you'd never master. Enjoy the pleasure of your own company. Every day, pleasure yourself somehow: fresh flowers, a long, hot bath, a meal you make just for the sheer pleasure. Learn to receive pleasure as readily as you give it. Say *Please, please me,* and then let the pleasuring begin!

Ponder

Stop thinking so hard and ponder instead. Reflect and consider and take all the time you want. Turn a question over and over in your mind; see it forward and backward and upside down and from the inside out. Let it roll around in your mind, in your heart, in your belly. Ponder the decisions you've made in your life—don't analyze. Ponder why you feel betrayed by those you trusted most—don't intellectualize. Ponder the choices you make when it comes to relationships—don't try to psychoanalyze. Sit and ponder without feeling the need to careen toward some self-imposed finish line. Say *Hmmmm* often when you ponder. Ask yourself

> *Could I be . . . ?*
>
> > *Is it possible that I've . . . ?*
> >
> > *Should I consider . . . ?*

Be content not to know, just to wonder, just to ponder.

Practice

Practice what you preach. Practice nonviolence—and that includes spiders. Practice nonjudgment—and that includes women on death row. Follow some sort of meditative or contemplative practice. Practice yoga, meditation, or simply practice sitting still. Know that it's more about practice than it is about perfect. Take up a musical instrument and love it so much that you'll want to practice every day. Turn off the computer and practice your penmanship (watch your descenders). Seek out a law practice that practices justice for all. Practice kindness, practice peace. Practice common sense and common courtesy, and know that you have practiced well.

Praise

Raise yourself up with praise. Give praise for fresh tomatoes in the summer, butternut squash in the fall, and garlic all year round. Give praise for baby ducks in the spring. Give praise for getting through the darkness and coming into the light. You decide who or what gets your praise, and where, and how. Sing praises, speak them, blow them through a trumpet. Praise that young woman or man who faced a tough decision and did the right thing. Let her know it matters. Let him know, too. Praise honesty, dignity, integrity, and compassion when you see them in action. Praise yourself for taking the risk, for choosing love over fear, for staying with your own truth when everyone tried to shoot you down. Praise a child twenty times for every one time you criticize. Praise yourself for remembering to give praise.

Pray

Pray when you need something and when you don't. Pray out loud or pray silently. Pray with others or pray alone. Pray outside, inside, or somewhere in between. Think of it as another kind of conversation, another way to talk with Spirit, Goddess, God, Jesus, Mary, Buddha, Mother Earth, Mohammed, Whoever you choose. Pray in the way that feels right for you. Sit down, stand up, kneel, lie down, dance. Chant, tone, drum, sing, speak. Pray that you'll be granted wisdom, courage, faith, healing. Pray for your highest good. Pray for others, those you know and those you don't. Remember to pray when things are going well and you are grateful. Never underestimate the power of prayer. Blessed be. A ho.

Amen.

Protect

Above all, protect what truly matters. Protect yourself from people who would steal your freedom. Protect yourself from situations that are guaranteed to bring you down. If you have the chance, protect one human being from persecution. Protect one hundred. Stop trying to protect your child from every scrape and bruise in life: you'll never do it. Stop trying to protect others' feelings with half-truths: you serve no one. Protect a grandmother elm that deserves to live. Protect a tiny fish that wants to swim. Protect your home from too much television, too much technology. Protect whatever pockets of peace you may find, wherever you may find them. And when you're not up to the task, ask that others more powerful protect them for you.

Prove

Prove to yourself that you can do it. Prove that you were always who you thought you were, not who they said you had to be. Prove to yourself that you're as mechanically minded as the next person. That you can do numbers, that you can fix engines, that you can design a new room and build it and wire it and paint it and decorate it and fill it with cushions and curtains and love. Prove once and for all that you're not just smart—you're brilliant. Prove that it's no crime to be sensitive, to be sexy, to be strong. Lay to rest the question of whether you're a real artist, a real writer, a real thinker, a real healer, a real athlete, a real mother, a real woman. Prove it to yourself and prove it to the world. Then let go of your need to prove.

Purge

Hold the Mother of All Yard Sales
and get rid of everything you don't
really need or don't truly adore.
Whittle away at your possessions
year after year, so they never have
the chance to possess you. Drink
more water than you ever thought
possible. Then drink some more.
Purge yourself of old ways that get
in the way of creating new. Purge
yourself of self-destructive habits
and arrogance. Clean out a drawer,
a closet, a shelf, or any part of yourself that's crammed too full with too
much. Only when the glass is empty
can you fill it up again.

Push

Sometimes now and then, you've just got to push. Push yourself to make it over the finish line. Push yourself to make your deadline. Push yourself up over Heartbreak Hill. Push yourself to stand without crutches. Push yourself to try! Come on, push a little harder. Push your body. Push your brain a little further. Push the limits of your endurance. Dig way down deep and push. Roll back the stone that's blocking your way. Push! Push through the roadblocks—real or imagined—that say you can't make it. Push! Push past indecision and confusion. Push on. Push yourself to get it done. Come on, push just a little harder. Everybody's pulling for you, now *push!*

Put

Put 'er there! Put your hand in the hand.
Put up with the put-downs for only so
long, and then put your convictions on the
line. In life as in poker, put up or shut up.
Put your money where your mouth is.
Never put off 'til tomorrow what you
should have done last Wednesday. Put
yourself in her place. Put yourself in his
shoes. Put two and two together. Put in
your two cents (which, allowing for infla-
tion, now equals about a buck twenty). Put
your money on a long shot. If you can't
afford it, put your collection of antique
thimbles up for sale. Don't put all your
eggs in one basket. Put away the dishes and
put out the cat. Then put the kids down
and you can put out the light.

Putter

Do a lot of nothing at all. Rearrange your
books, your CDs. Put them in alphabetical
order. No, arrange them by categories, or try
color coding. Walk around your garden with a
trowel in your hand. Maybe pull a few weeds or
turn a little dirt. Oh, maybe not. Hang that old
picture of your grandmother over by the window. No, over in the hall. Well, maybe stand it
on a table. Throw out some personal papers.
Oops, recycle them instead. Oh my, first separate out the white ones. Try doing something
different with your hair. Yikes, try again! Read
that new book you just got from the library. Oh
wait, finish that other book first. While you're
looking for it, find those old letters you wanted
to answer. Search for that pen you like so much.
Put on water for tea. But first, a little snack . . .

Quench

Quench every thirst you have. Start with a tall, cool glass of pure water. Drink it all. Quench your thirst for life by getting out and living! Quench your thirst for adventure, quench your thirst for passion. If you have a thirst to be with people, go out and meet some. Have a thirst for your own business? Go out and start one. Before you're too dried up, before the dryness sets in so deep you can hardly last another minute, quench your thirst to be on center stage. Thirsting for spiritual understanding? Seek it. Thirsting for greater connection with the universe? Uncover it. Thirsting for love? Give some. Thirsting for more meaningful relationships? Co-create some. Drink from cups of loving kindness, deep wells of wisdom, rivers of self-knowledge, pitchers of humility. Drink until you're full and moist and flowing and fertile. Then go back and drink some more.

Question

Never stop asking. Ask who you are, why you're here, what your life's purpose is all about—and be perfectly content not to know any of the answers. Ask *Why me? Why her? Why not them?* Question your motives and those of others. Is your intention pure? Question why the woman down the street with yellow curtains at her window makes you remorseful about your younger sister. Just question; the answer may take months or years to present itself. Question why others have what you so desperately want—and then question why you so desperately want it. Sit with not knowing, as difficult and frustrating as it feels. Sit. Without questions, how will you ever stumble onto any answers? Don't rush toward resolution. At the heart of every question lies a greater quest.

Quit

Quit when it's quitting time. When you can no longer see straight, call it quits for the night. When you're getting absolutely nowhere, quit traveling the same rocky road to the same dead end. Quit going back to the well when you know the well is empty. If your job is making you crazy, don't wait until you have another one before you quit. When you've had it up to here with her nonsense, quit being available every time she calls, no matter when she calls. Full? Quit eating. Sick of their rude and ignorant questions? Quit answering. If the meetings bore you, quit going. If you bore yourself, quit staying home alone all the time. Quit your complaining and quit making excuses! Quit expecting him to change, and quit resisting a change in yourself. Quit thinking you're a quitter if you quit now and then. If they tell you you *are*, quit listening!

Rage

Rage when your anger has built up, layer upon layer, year after year after angry, resentful year. Have a rage-fest deep in the forest, where no one will hear you. Pound your fists into a pillow; pick up your axe and chop wood. Express your rage by running hard and fast, pounding the pavement with every step and blowing off steam with every breath you take. Throw rocks if you can do it without harm to yourself or others. Jump rope, play the piano loudly and powerfully. Rage at your parents, your bosses past and present, everyone who ever loved you and left—or who never loved you at all. Rage at the hatred and injustice in the world, at the pain and suffering. At *your* pain and suffering. If anyone suggests that your rage is unladylike, irrational, or downright inappropriate, tell him to *Get lost!* and get on with your rage.

Raise

Raise yourself up from wherever you came from. Raise children who know the difference between right and wrong. Raise African violets that know precisely when to bloom. Raise your voice in song and raise the rafters. If it's your thing, raise the spirits of the dead. Put out your hand and help raise up another woman. Raise yourself up out of ignorance. Raise yourself out of the past and into the light of today. When there's no other way—and you've tried them all—raise a fuss right there at City Hall. Raise the roof of your front porch when it starts to sag. Raise miniature poodles, raise tropical fish, raise chickens. Raise your consciousness by spending time with people who are raising theirs. Raise your voice if you think it will make a difference. When hatred and violence threaten, raise yourself up to your full height and raise a flag for goodness and truth.

Rake

Rake the golden, red leaves of autumn into big, billowy piles, and don't forget to jump into them until you have twigs in your hair and you can't stop laughing. Rake with long, slow strokes. Rake until the rake scrapes along the bare dirt and glides over the long grass still wearing summer's green. Like a Zen monk, rake tiny pebbles into spirals, white waves, concentric circles, designs of quiet contemplation. Rake in rows; rake in the shape of your name. Let the rake lead the way. Rake out that corner of your yard where stones and stalks and cones have piled up helter-skelter. Dodge the roly-poly bugs and the fat and sassy earthworms. Hum a little tune while you rake, while you rake, while you rake to the rhythm of the rake.

Reach

Reach a little farther inside every day. Go deeper, try to reach your innermost core. Reach for a star, reach for the moon. If you can't quite reach your goal, consider moving it a little closer. Consider asking someone to give you a boost. Consider reaching in a whole new way. When you've reached the end of your rope, reach for a pair of scissors. Reach for the earth at least as often as you reach for the sky. Reach over and help a woman who's struggling. Remember that when you reach the mountaintop, there's a valley on the other side. Then there's another mountain. Proceed on your way without ever caring if you reach your destination. Know that everything humanly possible is within your reach, no matter what. When you think you've reached the end, reach out and touch a brand-new beginning.

Read

Start reading when you're a young girl, and never stop. Read stories and poems and essays and limericks and greeting cards and pamphlets. Read things by rich and famous writers; read things by everyone else, too. Read your favorite words out loud to your favorite woman. Lie on a blanket at the shore just after the sun has dipped down, and read out loud to each other. Read signs and labels if they're useful. Read speeches and manifestos if they stir your passions. (If not, recycle them immediately.) Read along with the congregation. Read the fine print. Don't read it just because the *New York Times* told you to. (Consider reading it because Oprah told you to.) Read everything you've written yourself, and save it. After fifteen years, go back and read it again. If anyone tries to stop you from reading, read them the riot act.

Rebel

When you just can't swallow what you're being fed, rebel. Proudly, openly, loudly rebel. When Paris dictates short skirts and fishnet hose, flip them the bird and wear your skirts long and your legs bare. When some government scientists announce that green salads are no longer good for you, tell them to take a hike and have yourself an extra head of romaine for lunch. Rebel against self-anointed, so-called authorities who proclaim books you *must* read, movies you *must* see, personalities you *must* be fascinated with, and causes you *must* support. Rebel, rebel, rebel, rebel. Fight back against ridiculous ordinances, outdated and restrictive Victorian social mores, stupid rules, and slipshod products. Let them know you're not about to put up with it, and *yes, thank you very kindly*, you *will* make waves, and you *will* rebel.

Receive

For once, stop giving, giving, giving to everyone but yourself. Be open to what comes your way—and be none too hasty to turn it aside. Accept a compliment, a gift, a favor, with grace. Purge *Oh, you shouldn't have!* from your vocabulary. Receive the love that others offer, in whatever form it takes. Voice what you need—be it a hug, a moment of talk, food for your table, a loan of money—and know that it will be provided. Loosen your white-knuckled, stressed-out grasp on life and then let the palms of your hands fill to overflowing. Know that you deserve all you receive, and remember to show your gratitude for the sheer magnificence of a life lived well.

Refuse

Refuse to be bullied, negated, or dishonored. Hold your ground when those who are different or in positions of power want to push you around. When the man behind the desk treats you like a child, just say *No*. When a friend lays her guilt or his insecurities or their stuff on you, refuse to own it. Refuse to be the last one to get her needs met. Refuse to let go of your fondest dreams and desires. At every opportunity, turn down shame or blame thrown in your direction. Stop doing what causes you pain. Just refuse to continue. Stomp your feet if you must. Scream and yell if you must. Refuse with your deepest truth, that which you know is real and right and good—and just say *No* to anything else.

Rekindle

When you believe something has gone out for good, rekindle it. Rekindle the hope you thought you had lost. Rekindle the love you were certain had died. Rekindle the magic. Fan the blackened embers of your own creativity and welcome back your inner fire. Rekindle your love of music; just start playing whatever instrument you can get your hands on. Rekindle your love of the outdoors; just put on hiking boots and go! Rake away the charred remains of your past and rekindle the wonder that (*Yes!*) lives on in your childlike heart. Find the tiniest spark, even though it seems impossible. Fuel the flame, even though it seems hopeless. Know that the human spirit is nearly inextinguishable—and like the Phoenix, you will rise free and proud from the ashes again.

Release

Let go of anybody or anything that holds you back or holds you down. Release the tension you've been carrying in your neck and shoulders for you-don't-know-how-long. Find a body-worker to help you. Release the anger you've stored up inside you since you were eleven years old. Find a therapist to guide you. Release the inner critic who says you have to do everything to perfection. Admit you can't do it alone and seek out someone to help. Let go of old rage, ancient resentments, and old beliefs that you'll never have enough or do enough or be enough. Now that you're grown, release that little-girl need to please mommy and daddy, and start pleasing yourself. Release yourself from the chains of the past so you can ease lightly into the gift that is your present.

Relish

Eat it up!

Eat it *all* up!

Relish every last morsel of every last bite of every delight. Relish the thought of being with someone you love—and then relish every moment together. Relish a cool, drenching rain after a blistering day. Take your clothes off and relish every drop. Relish a plate of English shortbread; relish every crumb. If you've earned it, relish the limelight. If you deserve it (and you'll know if you do), relish the respect. Relish the total, utter silence. Relish the sight of spring's first robin. Relish the summer's last rose. Relish the first day of school. Relish the last. Yes, yes, relish a good hot dog, all slathered and covered with . . .

Remember

Remember who you are and where you came from. Don't forget to remember the pain. Remember how it felt the first time you kissed somebody full on the mouth. Remember being so scared you peed in your pants. Remember that day you hoped would never end. Remember when it did. Remember when you were so free and alive that nothing could stand in your way. Then, suddenly, everything could. Remember when they wouldn't believe you. Remember when your mother died, or when her mother died, or when a child you didn't even know died. Remember when parts of yourself died— or when you put them on a shelf so high you couldn't reach them. Now remember how to get them back. Do you remember?

Rendezvous

After work, rendezvous. Before the concert begins, rendezvous. Rendezvous in the parking lot before and after school. Rendezvous just where the old post road turns to gravel. Rendezvous before dawn. Catch first light together, high up enough to see it rise over the plain. Meet at dusk; rendezvous with snowshoes and ragg mittens and strong coffee. Rendezvous at the lake for fishing, at the spa for foot reflexology. Rendezvous beneath the weeping willow on the north side of town. Everyone leave at five-twenty on Friday, and rendezvous at the first stop on the interstate. Meet in the lobby, gather on the corner, assemble peacefully in front of the plant, inside the ice-cream shop, out back of the barn. Remember you have a rendezvous with destiny, and remember to be on time.

Renew

Renew your passion for being alive! Visit a museum and renew your love of history. Renew that excitement you used to feel whenever you saw something Aztec, something Japanese, something from a distant time. Renew your spirit. Take a long walk, a short trip, a week's retreat. Forget to take your appointment book and your reading file. Renew your relationship to your body. Go to the gym, go on a backcountry ski trip, go get shiatsu, go do yoga. Renew old friendships. Renew that spark that used to live between the two of you. Renew your vows, the promises you made to yourself and others long ago. Start over, start again, start anew. Revive, restore, refresh, replenish.

Rejuvenate,

recharge,

and

renew.

Resist

Resist the urge to be anything other than who you truly are. When you find yourself playing games you never thought you would, resist. When temptation invites you to take just one drink, just one hit, just one more piece of cake, resist. Resist the seductive pull of low-interest, no-obligation credit cards that are neither. Resist any attempt—no matter how subtle—to suppress your creative expression. When they try to drag you into their web of negative thinking and limited beliefs, resist. With all your might, resist any and all efforts to control the way you walk or cook or clean or socialize. Simply insist, *I must resist.*

Respect

Respect yourself, and insist that others do the same. Respect your own need for privacy, for peace and quiet. Lock the bathroom door if you must. Respect the limitations of your own mortality. Respect the process when it's working; withdraw your respect when it goes awry. Respect the fact that a world filled with light will also include the darkness; that a day of joy can be followed by a day of unfathomable misery. Even when you don't like something, don't agree with it, you can respect it. Respect all your elders. Respect this tired planet we call home. Whatever your beliefs, respect a woman's right to choose her own. To gain my respect, offer yours in return.

Respond

When someone asks, answer. When someone looks into your eyes, look back. When something touches you, be touched. Respond to kindness in kind. Respond to threats with courage; respond to oppression with outrage. Respond to a genuine compliment with a genuine *Thank you.* Respond in the moment—not days later with a chorus of *I should have, I could have, Why didn't I . . . ?* Increase your response-ability. Respond with love when you feel loved. Respond with very clear and precise boundaries when you feel violated. Respond according to how you truly feel, not according to what you think is acceptable. Never apologize for your responses, as long as they are authentic and expressed with pure intention. If repeated attempts elicit no response from another human being, respond with your feet and walk away.

Rest

Take five. **Take a catnap.** Take a break. Rest. Turn off the computer, turn off the lights, turn off the phone, and rest. Bring it all to a slow and quiet halt. For a little while, rest. Ask someone else to cover for you while you rest. **Listen to soothing music** while you rest. The work will get done in its time if you rest. The children can occupy themselves while you rest. While you wait for the water to boil, rest your feet. While you wait for your date to show up, rest your eyes. No one is watching the clock, so just rest. **When you're weary** to the core, it's your soul that needs rest. When your energy flags, give your body some rest. The permission is there; now just take it and rest. The rest of the world will go on while you rest.

Restore

Put something back together so it's
stronger and more beautiful than it was
before. Put that rosy glow back into your
cheeks. Rub and polish the front hall
floor until it's as grand as it once was.
Take apart a chair, a coat, a carburetor,
and bring it back just the way it was, only
different this time. Only better. Do the
same with your health, your attitude
about others, or those pottery shards that
were once a pitcher. Reconstruct that
which you want to hold fast; deconstruct
that which you want to see crumble to
pieces. If your home or your neighborhood has become a battlefield, try to
restore peace and order wherever you can.
Restore your faith in humanity, and
restore your faith in yourself.

Resume

Go back and pick up where you left off.
No matter how long it's been, no matter
how unkind the words, resume contact.
Pick up the thread that you may have
dropped along the way. Remember when
you always had time to sit on the porch
and visit? Remember the times you and
your girlfriends whispered and laughed
like seventh graders—even though you
were well into your forties? Resume those
times. Go back and pick up the thread
you dropped along the way. Even if you
took time out to go to college, to run a
business, to raise three children, to build a
village—now you can resume all the
things you stopped doing along the way.
The thread remains. Go back and pick it
up *now* and resume your course for living.

Retreat

Retreat from the hundreds of daily details that pull you in all directions. Skip the committee meeting. Let the phone tree wait. Send everyone away for the day and revel in the bliss of being alone in your own home. Get out of town to a place— anyplace!—where no one knows you. Hide in the stacks at the library; sit on the floor in a corner and look at picture books. Find solace in a spot of green, a stand of trees, a bit of water, a heavenly spot you create in your mind. Don't make excuses. Retreat to the bathtub, to your bedroom, to your car if you must. Drive and drive and pull off the road when you've driven exactly far enough. Make time, make space to do nothing at all. Remove the outside stimuli that pound at you endlessly. Tell people you've left town; then lower the shades and stay exactly where you are. Resist the urge to do something or be somewhere. After you've gotten the hang of it, re-treat yourself more often.

Return

Go back to something you lost somewhere along the way. Go back to being a red-head; go back to wearing the kinds of dresses that make you want to dance. Return to school and get a degree or a certificate. Or don't. Go back to one of the places you used to live. Walk by. Sit across the street and watch people come and go. Visit the woman you used to see every day but haven't seen for fifteen years. Retrace a trip you once took. See yourself through new eyes. You decide what you still want from that time—and what you don't want. Return to a happier time, a more satisfying time, a time of great wonder. For every turn you take, make at least one re-turn.

Reveal

As much or as little as you wish, reveal.
One veil at a time, one layer at a time,
reveal your true nature. Reveal the truth
in proper doses at the proper time.
Reveal only as much of the story as you
feel compelled to reveal. And only to
those worthy of the revelation. Reveal
no secrets you were asked to conceal.
Ask for guideposts along the way, and,
in their time, they will be revealed to
you. Look to the source for divine inspiration and it, too, will be revealed. Trust
another human enough to reveal your
darkest longings. Trust her to reveal her
own. Let your walk reveal your authentic self; let your actions reveal the
strength of your will.

Revel

Kick up your heels, bay at the moon, dance under the stars. Sing to the heavens, sing to the Earth. Join hands and circle around, circle around, until you fall in joyous ecstasy. Revel in the rain, dripping and soaking until you finally peel off your sopping clothes. Revel in the sunshine, skipping through the flower-strewn meadows, holding buttercups under your chin and stringing sweet clover chains. Revel with other women, skirts twirling and hips swirling, cheeks glowing and hair flowing. Celebrate all there is and all that has yet to be. Drink homemade berry wine and eat cakes in deliciously provocative shapes. Revel all night long, twinkling with the stars, and when the sun peeks over the horizon in the morning, rise up and revel again.

Reward

Give yourself something that makes you smile. A chocolate kiss, an afternoon with absolutely nothing to do. Reward yourself for a job well done. Reward yourself for getting through a horrible night. Take a dollar or five or five hundred and reward yourself for being brave, for being beautiful, for closing the big sale, for finishing what you started. Better yet, reward yourself for nothing in particular, for just being you. Reward yourself for letting the house go without cleaning, for letting the laundry sit an extra day. Pick yourself a bouquet of flowers at the market or, better yet, send flowers to yourself. Remember to write a lovely note and sign it *Me.*

Ripen

Give yourself plenty of time to get ripe and ready. Ripen naturally at your own speed, your own rhythm. Ripen when you're forty-three or fifty-one or seventy-eight. Ripen to a full-bodied bouquet that younger women can only imagine. Watch yourself ripening over the years, and revel in it. Ripen with dignity, with joy, with anticipation of the days when you are fully ripe. Appreciate the signs of ripening: the insight, the wisdom, the patience, the look in your eyes that says *Honey, I've been there and I know what it's about.* Ripen to perfection, juicy and luscious and oh so tender to the touch. Like a fine wine, a juicy, sweet strawberry, a cheese that's richer for its years, you'll be utterly delicious when you're ripe.

Rise

Rise up to your highest potential and help others rise to theirs. When small-minded thinking and toxic opinions threaten to bring you down, rise above them. Rise up singing. Rise up in joy. Rise every morning grateful for the promise of a new day. Rise above what you thought were your ultimate limitations. Create a new, higher level of limitations, then rise above them, too. When idiots spew their hateful venom your way, rise above it. Take a higher road. Lighten your load of emotional baggage and rise above your nonproductive habits. Educate yourself so you can rise above ignorance. When you feel as though the muck and grime, the ooze and slime of every day could pull you down and hold you in its lowly clutches, be as light as a feather and rise.

Risk

Be willing to lose something in order to gain something else. Take an emotional risk: say *I love you and want to be with you.* Take a financial risk: invest in a woman-owned business or a community-supported farm. Take a creative risk: pick up a paintbrush or a violin; go to the contact improvisation dance class; show your poems to somebody. Be willing to show your vulnerabilities: cry. Take the risk and show more power than you've shown before: insist! Risk everything, and if you lose it all, realize how much richer you are for it. Risk being laughed at, risk being heckled, risk being silenced. Risk being hurt. Risk being more joyful, more brilliant, more alive, and more filled with the Bliss Goddess than you've ever imagined. Only when you're ready to risk losing it all can you risk having it all—and more.

Rock

Keep moving to the rhythm of the Earth. Rock a baby until her eyelids flutter and close. Rock gently side to side in the grocery line. Rock till dawn in a dress that lets you move in nine directions. Go to a church that rocks, join a band that rocks. Always have at least one rocking chair, with an afghan nearby. Find an old porch swing and rock in it until the houses and trees slip away and you become only rock. When you're pulled in all directions, rock yourself back to center. Feel yourself in the arms of someone larger, vaster, wiser, and more loving than anyone you know. Let her rock you, rock you, rock you through your darkness and confusion, and return you to a place where your footing is solid as a rock.

Roll

Roll down a grassy slope at least three times each year. Roll skeins of yarn into firm balls whether you're knitting or not. Roll rice in sheets of nori; add a steamed carrot and a bit of avocado. Roll up pairs of socks when they come out of the dryer. Then roll them down the hall and let the cat have a ball. Roll out piecrusts, roll up stuffed cabbage, roll cookies in powdered sugar. Slap on some in-line skates and roll! Step onto your teenager's skateboard and roll! Go to Las Vegas and roll the dice if you feel like it. Roll around on the floor and loosen up your spine after sitting all day. When one of your kids rolls her eyes at you, roll yours right back. Collect all the spare pennies around the house, roll them in wrappers, and treat yourself to an iced chai tea and a chocolate chip cookie. If you have lots of penny rolls, treat someone else, too.

Never quit when you're on a roll!

Satisfy

Satisfy all your hungers—your hunger to love and be loved, your hunger to be touched in the most passionate way, your hunger to create, your hunger to understand. Feed them well and often. Satisfy your curiosity. Ask lots of questions, and don't stop asking until you're satisfied with the answers. Satisfy all your desires. Do it before you satisfy everybody else's. Scratch the itch that's been bugging you all these years. The itch to graduate, the itch to take the controls of a plane in flight, to belly dance, to reach the summit of Denali. Satisfy that powerful urge to start a fresh, new page in your life or an entire new chapter. Stop searching for that one person who can satisfy your every need. You'll never find that person, and if you did, you'd never be satisfied, anyway.

Savor

Slow down and enjoy every taste, every smell, every experience. Linger over tea for at least two hours and forty-seven minutes. Give yourself thirty-nine bites to make your way through a chocolate bar. Read the poem you love word by word, letter by letter. Read it again even more slowly. Give a child one more twirl; give yourself two more moments of quiet reflection. Why rush indoors when you can feel a warm rain tickle your face? Why keep driving when the sun is setting out one window and the moon is rising out the other? Why plow through life when you can take in as much as you can? You can't always save a moment in time, but you can savor it.

Say

Say *I love you.* Say *I don't.* Say *I want to*; say *I won't.* Say *I'm sorry, I forgive you, I miss you.* Say *I need you to be more honest with me.* Say *I need your help.* Say *Thank you, I don't need your help.* Say *Your hair is beautiful, your dress is pretty. You're looking great.* Say *No, I don't want that; yes, I want that there.* Say *I don't know exactly what to say.* Say *Hello* and smile. Say *Goodbye.* Say what you mean. Say what you must say. Say *I am not the source of your pain.* Say *I am so very proud of you.* Say *I am so happy you are part of my life.* Say exactly as much as needs to be said. Then don't say another word.

Scandalize

Yes, once in a while, give 'em something to talk about! Tell good taste to take a flying leap and wear that dress you swore would never leave your bedroom. Sit on the floor at the movies, eat with your fingers (messily), sing off-key as loudly as you can. Disagree when everyone else is agreeing. Laugh out loud when everyone else is quietly frowning. Make noise, make waves, and make love on the back porch in the middle of the afternoon alongside the walking trail. If you're new at this, start small. Have a different flavor of yogurt for lunch. Try on that pair of lacy underpants at the lingerie store. Shake 'em up a little, then when you're ready, scandalize!

Sense

Sharpen your sense of everything. The minute you walk into the room, sense that something isn't quite right. Listen to her voice on the phone, and sense that she is mouthing someone else's words. Sense that she may be in danger. Have a sixth sense about this particular relationship—even though it appears perfect on the surface. Sense that the woman in the back office is troubled. Sense that she needs a friend with a strong shoulder, and be that friend. Sense that things may not be all they seem. Suss it out. Meet someone for the first time and sense that there's some kind of intense connection between you that you can't name. Sense that you are becoming more attuned to everything around you. When people say *Oh, don't be so sensitive*, sense that you've scared them clean out of their senses.

Separate

When you start to lose yourself in another person, put some distance between you. Separate when you're fused at the hip and can no longer go your own ways. Separate for a day, for a week-end, for a month, or for a year. Move to separate corners, separate bedrooms, separate houses, separate countries. Consider that you just might have to separate for good. Separate and come back together in a new way, with new ground rules and new boundaries. Separate bit by bit from your children before the apron strings are so knotted you can't get them undone. Separate whenever staying together is too difficult, too draining, too dangerous for your body, mind, or psyche. Separate when the pain of being together is greater than the pain of being apart.

Serve

Serve a higher purpose. Serve humanity, serve the Earth, serve the greater common good. Dedicate your life to service in its many forms. Serve in your own way, using the precious gifts that only you can give. Serve the young, the old, the dying. Serve women, serve men, serve to bring us closer together. Serve families formed by birth, choice, or circumstance. Serve the very weak, serve the strong and powerful. Serve through medicine, through law, through laughter and song. Through deeds, through words, by the sweat of your brow and the love in your heart. Serve in whatever way you are called to serve. Serve others with no concern for serving yourself, and know you will always be served.

Settle

When things are unsettling, settle down. Settle in on a snowy Sunday with a cup of something warm and a to-do list that's as empty as the icy streets. Find a house or an apartment or a tipi and settle in enough so that you feel like you're at home. Settle long enough to put up a curtain or two, long enough that the mail carrier knows your name. Settle for nothing less than magnificence. Settle out of court whenever you can—it's much more humane. Settle up your debts as quickly and cleanly as you can. Do it in your own way, with as much integrity as you can muster. Settle down into a comfortable chair and exhale slowly. Put another log on the fire, and settle in for a long winter's nap. Don't settle for anything—*anything!*—less than you truly deserve.

Shampoo

Shampoo your hair in the dark, before the sun is up. Feel it fall between your fingers, wet and silken and shapeless, tangled, coarse, ringlets on your forehead. Slowly massage your scalp, every bump and hollow on your head. Shampoo someone in bed without dropping a single drop. Imagine you are a mermaid, Rapunzel, Medusa if you must. You are on the rocks, you are in the tower, and your hair goes on forever. Shampoo the peach fuzz hair of a newborn, shampoo the wispy, angelic threads of one who is soon to die. Give the shampoo person at the salon a few extra dollars to give you a few minutes more. Drop your head into his hands. Let your beloved shampoo your hair, anointing you with berries, chamomile, madder root, coconut, lemon. When your hair is clean, you can meet the world anew.

Shape

Feel your fingers pulling, rolling, pinching, coiling, making shapes. With clay, beeswax, the children's Play-Doh, something you rustle up from flour and baking soda and cream of tartar. Flex your fingers, press your thumbs, unleash the art in your knuckles, nails, palms of your hands. Nests are easy; fill them with tiny eggs. Spotted snakes slither across the kitchen table. Tiny baskets overflow with mini-zucchini, great cobs of corn, and peas nestled in their cozy pods. Shape bread and rolls, cookies without cutters. Form Celtic knots, braids, pinwheels, anatomically correct Hims and Hers. Remind your hands that some muscles are not there solely to hold a pen, ring up a phone number, drive a car, operate a computer. Shape your world with your own two hands, and watch a new world begin to take shape.

Share

No matter how little you have or how much, share it. Give your last drops of lavender bath oil to a friend who needs the relaxation more than you do. Share your gift of song, your smile, your recipe for falafel. Share your "first time" experiences with a younger woman; share your thirst for understanding with an older woman. Never stop sharing. Share a sunny afternoon, a rainy morning, a quiet sunrise, your last Sunday before returning to school. Share your home with someone who doesn't have one right now. Share your clothes. Break your cookie into pieces and share them with everyone at the table. You *are* as you *share*. If you have a hundred dollars, share twenty-five. If you have one dollar, share twenty-five cents. Drop your scarcity mind-set. Even when you think you have barely enough, you always have something to share.

Shave

If it makes you feel happy, do it.
If it makes you feel like a slave
to a male-dominated view of
beauty, don't.

End of discussion.

Shed

Slip out of anything that no longer fits. Wiggle
your way out of old habits, old patterns, old
friendships that pinch in all the wrong places.
Shed your skin like a snake and allow a glistening new outer wrap to come to the surface.
Drop that tired, old way of reacting to criti-
cism. Shed the mask of cool, controlled perfection. Get rid of that insincere smile, that
affected way you cock your head when you're
pretending to listen to whoever's talking. They
never worked anyway. Shed any belief—no
matter how long you've held onto it—that gets
in the way of your own magnificence. Shed
about five-and-a-half inches of that dry, brittle
hair; shed those eleven pounds you've been carrying around for—*what was the reason*? When
something's dead, you need to shed.

Shift

Shift your consciousness. See circles instead of boxes, see rolling hills instead of straight lines. Shift your very way of looking at things. See webs of interconnectedness with no one on top and no one on the bottom. Shift your orientation. See families of all shapes, sizes, colors, and persuasions. Shift your perspective. Rethink your views on people, on institutions, on social issues. Shift. Move over a hair and stand outside and beside yourself. Watch how you take in information; watch your immediate reaction to familiar things. Now in the smallest way, shift. Imperceptibly shift. Then watch everyone else around you shifting, too.

Show

Show your stuff. Show another woman the way
to show hers. Show a side you never showed
anyone before. For the first time, show a friend
the scar from that horrible, horrible night. Show
who you are through writing, art, movement.
When someone says *This is the way!*, show them
another. Show restraint when you feel your center being pulled away from you. Show a bit of
compassion every day. If you've committed a
wrong, show remorse. Be sure to feel it first.
Show someone how glorious life can be, simply
by living a glorious life. Show the world what a
woman looks like, acts like, and is. Show yourself. Show as much skin as you like. Or as little.
If they don't like it, show them the door.

Sift

Imagine all the possibilities of your life in one large, glorious pile. Now start sifting. Painstakingly examine each grain, each morsel. Do you want it? Need it? Does it serve you? Decide what stays, what goes, what gets folded in together. Sift slowly and mindfully. It may take months or years. Or your entire life. Once you've sifted things into neat piles, start the process all over again. Sift and resift, sift and resift. Wheat from chaff, sand from jewels, truth from illusion. Let the insignificant details fall through to the ground, leaving what's solid, what matters, behind.

Sigh

Sometimes you simply must sigh. When no words can capture the sweet, soulful breath escaping your lips, you simply must sigh. Sound a little hum when you sigh. Sigh when you know exactly what your friend means, yet words would cheapen the depth of her sentiment. Sigh when you want to respond but you're too weary, too spent to form words, much less sentences. Sigh when you massage a woman, solely to induce her sighing, too. Sigh when you hear violin music that seeps into your soul. Sigh at funerals just to keep breathing. Sigh when someone really needs more than anything to talk—and you need more than anything to listen. Smile a soft smile when you sigh. Never force a sigh. When you can sigh effortlessly at just the right moments, you will know that you are a woman, *sigh*, indeed.

Simplify

Do more with less. Better yet, do less. Schedule less, attend less—and be certain to leave long gaps of nothingness in your days and nights. Read less, reflect more. If you own two cars, figure out a way to get along with one. Then figure out a way to use it just three days a week. Have fewer, more genuine friends. Live simply so that others may simply live. Simplify your home. Have less furniture, and don't bother with anything you can't wipe with a damp rag. Turn down offers to get involved, no matter how great they sound. Stop lugging around all that junk in your purse! Simplify your wardrobe. Give away anything you don't actually wear, and make sure everything that's left can be worn together. Skip that whole shoe thing: have one pair for work, one for play, and one for slipping around in slimy creekbeds. Quit with the excuses already: it's simple to simplify.

Sing

Open your mouth and let your song escape! Sing on-key, off-key, no-key-at-all. Sing when you're happy, when you're sad, when you're vacuuming, and when you're walking. Sing anything you want. Sing the song that wells up in your heart. Sing the directions to your gynecologist's office. Sing your grocery list or the Old Testament or the names of all the women and men you know. Sing your anger—and make it as loud as you are angry! Sing a song of yesterday or of tomorrow. Sing your way into a different mood, or deeper into the one you're already in. Sing your life into existence. Every day, somehow, some way, however you can. Sing!

Sit

Sit cross-legged on the grass, under a shady tree. Sit alone without feeling lonely. Sit with children and marvel at all the questions they have; sit with elders and marvel at their wisdom. Sit somewhere different this time. Sit next to the person who makes you feel most nervous. Sit in the front row, where you thought you'd never sit. Sit in a chair by the window and when the phone rings, don't get up. Sit in a circle with other women—and with men. Get rid of your chairs and sit on the floor. Okay, go ahead and buy that twelve-hundred-dollar purple leather office chair with the built-in lumbar support, and feel like a queen every time you sit in it. Sit to meditate, sit to pray, sit to sing. Sit a little bit longer, a little bit quieter, than you sat yesterday. Sit on a bench at the art gallery and look at one painting for twenty-three minutes. Sit in silence. Sit as long as you need, and when it's time to stop sitting, stand.

Skip

Just once, skip a day of work. Skip a class. The world won't come to an end. Skip that monthly dinner that always bores you to the bone. Or go, but skip the cocktails and skip the vapid conversation. Skip coffee for a week, and see how you feel. At the next meeting, ask them to please skip the foolishness for once. Skip lunch now and then and go for a walk instead. Definitely consider skipping that extra piece of pie. Skip your weekly phone call to your mother (well, maybe not). Skip the dusting for two or three months and see if anyone notices. Skip a smooth, flat stone across a crystalline lake. Skip down the sidewalk with a child. Skip like Dorothy skipped in *The Wizard of Oz*. When someone asks why you're not acting your age, skip right over to them and say *Aw, skip it. Just skip it, will ya?*

Sleep

When your body cries out for sleep, give yourself as much as you need. Long twelve-hour stretches, if that's what's called for. Put a sleepy message on your voice mail. Let yourself go wherever sleep wants to take you. If you've been burning the candle at both ends, you eventually have to catch up. During the heaviest days of your period, sleep long. After you break your ankle or sprain your knee, sleep hard. Cry yourself to sleep if you need. Whatever's going on in the outside world, you can miss. Whoever needs desperately to reach you can wait. Give up the coffee and the soda and whatever other energy enhancers you've come to rely on, and reconnect with the sweet, awesome power of natural sleep.

Slow

What's the big hurry? Slow down. Where's
the fire? Slow down. Take it easy, take it
slow. Slow down when you drive, if you
really want to get there in one piece. Talk
low and talk slow, if you really want people
to hear you and understand. Stop running in
circles and slow the whole thing down.
Slowly but surely, you'll get it done. Put on
some slow music and slow dance. Take a
slow boat up the Amazon. Learn what it
means to have a slow hand. When things are
slow at work, call in sick. Call in slow. Like
the turtle, move slowly and live long. Slow
down enough to see what's passing you by.
Now go back and read this again, and this
time, go as slow as you can.

Smile

For no reason at all except that it will make you a happier person, smile. Smile at a perfect stranger, at your beloved, at a child whose adults are too busy or too preoccupied to smile. Show your teeth—especially if you haven't got any. Smile when you see someone or something you like. Smile broadly, demurely, shyly, mysteriously. Smile from ear to ear. Smile at the bus driver, smile at the toll taker, smile at the stressed-out driver at the stoplight. Make them all wonder, *What's she smiling about?* Let them wonder. Let a smile be your umbrella on a rainy day. Like the Cheshire cat, your smile will remain long after you're gone. You can travel miles on a smile.

Soften

Drop your shoulders and soften your stance. Be softer with yourself, more forgiving. Soften your approach. Allow yourself to be vulnerable, to be interdependent, to receive as well as give. Turn off the computer and write with a pencil, a piece of chalk, or a crayon. Try not to be so hard on yourself. Soften the shape of your body. Let those five or ten pounds come back and round out those boyish edges that are not at all becoming. Carry a woman's body. Speak a bit more softly; walk across the floor more softly. Wear something that flows: a skirt, a blouse, a dress, a scarf. Wrap a sarong around your middle. Resist the urge to sound like the men at the office or the boys in the class or the guys on the team. Give at least equal time to your softer, feminine nature, and feel its power. The power is yours when you soften.

Solo

Go it alone. Cycle across Canada by yourself. Solo. Backpack into the wilderness alone. Solo. Solo your way to the top of your field. Test the limits of your own independence. Solo your way to Singapore; solo your way across town. Be your own best friend. Solo. Buy a house by yourself; buy a car by yourself; buy a diamond ring by yourself. Solo Friday nights; solo Sunday mornings. Whatever it is, know that you can do it alone. Try it once, then know you can do it alone. Spend a week alone, talking to no one. Solo at the university; solo at your best friend's wedding; solo at the Thanksgiving table. Once you know you can solo, you'll know you can go it alone.

Solve

Figure it out. Come up with a solution that works. Once and for all, solve that persistent problem that's been nagging at you for—*could it be?*—years. Use logic, use intuition, use geometry. Rely on a calculator, a computer, the person who cuts your hair, or tea leaves in the bottom of your cup. Check out the I Ching. Pick all the pieces of the puzzle apart and then put them back together in a fresh, new way. Solve the mystery of how socks disappear in the dryer, how coat hangers breed in the night. Solve that thorny issue at work that's giving you constant indigestion. Be a sleuth or hire one. Be an oracle or consult one. Can you solve the anagram on this page? Work your brain, and when that isn't working, turn to your heart.

Sparkle

Shine and glitter and fill up a room with your glow. Paint your toenails and your fingernails with sparkles that catch the light of the moon. Wear silver earrings that sparkle, crystal and bead necklaces that sparkle and catch the light of the sun. Sparkle when you smile. (Go ahead and get your teeth bleached, if you want!) Wear a shirt covered with tiny mirrors. Wear shoes that throw rainbows around the room when you dance. Let your eyes sparkle when you see someone you love. Or someone you don't. Wear glittering makeup—as much as you want. Wear strands of stones, glass, or diamonds or paper covered with glitter—as many as you feel like! At the bank, sign your name with a pen that sparkles. Each day, look in a mirror that sparkles and remember it's a reflection of you.

Speak

When you have something to say, say it. Speak your mind and let your voice quiver and shake if it must. Speak what's in your heart and if you cry, so be it! When something is sitting on the tip of your tongue, let it out. Speak the truth that must be spoken— even if some will rail and flail against it. Have the courage to speak up. In whatever way you can, help others to have the courage, too. When it's impossible for others to speak on their own, speak on their behalf. Speak up for the animals, for the children, for the weak, for the sick. Remember to speak *for* as often as you speak *against*. Speak from a place deep inside, a place that knows what must be spoken. Keep speaking the truth and know that eventually, somehow, somewhere, someone will listen.

Spin

Crosspatch, draw the latch, sit by the fire and spin: Take a cup and drink it up, then call your neighbors in. Spin straw into gold; spin bees into honey. Spin a fine and fanciful tale, a yarn filled with twists and turns of plot and personality. Spin a ring around the moon. Spin around the sun and back again. To know the difference between the quiet rhythm of a spinning wheel and the jarring motion of spinning your wheels, spend an evening spinning with spinsters. Spin your own fate, weave your own web, and when you feel things spinning out of control, spin a silken cocoon and draw yourself in. While the world spins around you, spin your own sweet song.

Splash

Make a big splash, whatever you do. Splash cool, clear water on your face after a sweaty workout. Splash bits of fragrance here and there before a big evening. Splash bits of color all around your home: goldenrod on the doorjambs; hollyhock on the window frame; cornflower blue in drips and drabs on the drapes. Run barefoot through a public fountain and splash the people sitting dryly by. When they protest, splash them with your dazzling smile. Splash a bit of vanilla into your warm milk, a few drops of hazelnut liqueur onto your ice cream. Splash spaghetti sauce all over your white blouse, and then splash bleach on your black pants when you try to clean it up. Remember the time they splashed you in the water—only this time, remember to splash back!

Splurge

Go ahead, give yourself a little something extra. Nobody's looking—*and what if they are?* Just this once, buy the shampoo in the glass bottle with the ribbon around its neck. Have dessert before lunch, then have it again before dinner. Lounge in the bathtub for hours and let the telephone ring. Go to the flower shop and buy yourself a Bird of Paradise. Buy three. Pick out a sweater that isn't pre-worn or pre-owned or pre-anything. Buy underwear that doesn't have a "three-fer" price, that isn't 100 percent cotton. Skip the house wine and select something extravagant. Just this once. Sleep an extra half-hour. Sit through a double feature. What the heck, a triple feature. It's okay, really it is. You deserve it. If you've got the urge, splurge.

Squat

Plant your feet on the floor, on the earth, like birthing women do. Rest your elbows on your knees. Relax your knees. Let your energy drop down, down, out of your head. Let it fall below your belly. See how the world looks different when you're not so brain-heavy. Squat in the living room while you listen to music. Squat in the yard while you're picking aphids off the roses. Sway from side to side, from front to back. Or stay perfectly still. If you fall over, so what? Squat again. Now stay there. For five minutes, for an hour. Tomorrow, squat without underwear.

Squish

Take off your shoes and squish wet sand between every one of your toes. *Oooooh!* Pick up great gobs and globs and glubs of mud and squish them slowly between your fingers. *Oooooh!* Jump in a puddle, and feel the water squish through the holes in the seams of your boots. Squish your toothpaste out between your teeth and dribble it down your chin, and giggle all the while. Squish peanut butter all around your mouth. *Oooooh!* Squish cookie dough into some weird shapes, then roll it out and squish it again. Step in wet, squishy grass in squishy jelly shoes, and try not to step on squishy, jelly worms. *Ooooops!* Squish grapes and berries betwixt your toes in homemade wooden barrels.

Whatever you wish, squish!

Stand

Decide what you stand for and then stand up for it. Root yourself like a young tree, strong and supple and able to bend and flex when everything around you is flying by. Stand beside a young woman who's afraid. Stand in front of a child who needs protection. Stand tall and stand firm. Stand vigil late into the night, in the rain or the snow. Have the courage to stand alone and silent for what you know is right. Butterflies in your stomach are simply trying to lift you to your own two feet. Stand your ground as long and as often as you can—you'll know soon enough when it's time to sit down.

Stay

If you know it's not yet time to go, stay. Stay one more day. One more year. Stay for the duration. If you're not welcome, then stay out. If you have a right to be there, then stay. If you've lost your way, stay put. If you're frightened, ask someone to stay with you. This time, stay and help with the dishes. Next time, say *Sorry, but I can't stay another minute*. Stay true to your path, no matter how many others insist that you stay true to theirs. Stay awake, stay alive. Stay open to new possibilities you may never have considered. When you feel like dancing, stay out until dawn. When you're feeling vulnerable, stay home with the blinds drawn. In times of great struggle, stay close to each other and close to the earth, and peace will stay at your side.

Still

Quiet yourself. Beside a creek, parked outside your office, on a crowded street downtown. Still your body. Lie or sit or walk or float. You need not stand still to be still. Still your mind. Still the internal chatter that runs rampant in your head all day and half the night. Still the voices. Just change the channel. Bring yourself down, down to a place of peace. Focus only on your breathing. Breathing in, breathing out. Just for now, still your emotions. Let them rest. Still your heart if it's racing wildly. Still your thoughts of what was, what was not, and what might have been. Be the stillness. Be the stillness.

Still yourself.

Be still.

Stop

If it hurts, stop. Stop yourself before you've gone too far. Stop whining, stop kvetching, stop blaming anybody else for your problems. Stop and rest. Stop and take a few deep, long breaths. Stop running yourself ragged. Stop letting people use you. Just stop! Stop wasting anything—time, money, paper, food. For an hour, stop everything. Stop when you see red. Stop going out with people you dislike, to places you don't enjoy. Stop and smell the roses. The lavender. The lemons. Stop and say *Hello*. Stop waiting for your mother to fulfill some fantasy you've cultivated for thirty-five years—and start mothering yourself. Stop throwing away your right to vote. Stop waiting for miracles and start creating them. Ready, set, stop!

Strengthen

Make yourself strong. Build up your body so you can carry your own suitcase. It's never too late to start. Just do one step, one block, one mile, one repetition more than you did the day before yesterday. Strengthen your will so you can step out and do what needs to be done. Learn to carry your own weight and, if necessary, to carry others in their moments of weakness. Be strong enough to show your own weakness. (That's the greatest strength of all.) Be strong enough to ask for help when you need it. Have the courage to accept. Strengthen the muscles around your heart so you'll have the resiliency to hold others close and let them go all at the same time.

Stretch

Stretch your spine so you can move through life with greater flexibility. Be elastic enough to stretch without breaking. Stretch your vision to take in more of what you're now able to see. Go a little farther today than you did yesterday and then stretch a little more tomorrow. Stretch your beliefs and trust a little more. Stretch your faith and leap farther than you planned, sooner than you thought you could. Stretch your brain in new ways: next time, look at a problem upside down or from the inside out. Go somewhere you always wondered about but never felt you could go. Stretch yourself and go. When you're ready, stretch your boundaries and let another person get a little closer. Do that often. Pull back when you need to, and know that when it's time, you'll be ready to stretch again.

String

String a one-of-a-kind necklace just for you.
String wooden beads from Africa, jade rounds
from Mexico, tiny periwinkle shells, and Indian
trade beads. String the odds and ends you've
kept all these years. Pull apart that one stray ear-
ring, and string the lapis. String the tiny fetish,
the bear, the coyote, the fish. String slowly, letting the beads and charms and trinkets guide
you. String parts of yourself: your memories,
your scars. Your courage, your heart, your compassion, your strength. String a necklace that
only you can wear. String bells that ring, birds
that sing. When people exclaim *What a beautiful necklace!*, tell yourself *Aye, as beautiful as the
woman it encircles!*

Stroke

Stroke a cat under her chin and she's yours. Stroke a baby's cheek, circling gently until she drops off to sleep. See it work on grown-ups, too. During your father's last days, stroke his silver hair, the back of his thin and wrinkled hand. Stroke with firm tenderness a friend's forehead, bringing peace to her furrowed brow. Stroke your lover's thigh, of course. Tenderly stroke a velveteen pillow, a horse's neck, the valley of your own shoulder. Stroke a feather lightly over your belly and up between your breasts and behind your ears. In the water, stroke smoothly and with ease. In your bedroom, stroke wherever you please.

Struggle

Struggle to get where you want to be, and you will be the richer for it. Struggle to make ends meet and learn forever the value of what truly matters. Struggle to gain the freedom you deserve—and embrace freedom in your heart for all human beings, for all time. Fight tooth and nail to be heard, and never be silenced again. Get up early, stay up late, burn the candle at both ends, and you'll never waste another moment. Struggle against all odds. Provide for yourself even though they said you weren't smart enough; get your children back after five lawyers told you it was useless to try.

Struggle is never easy,
but it always makes you strong.

Support

Be there for another woman. Support her when no one else will. Support her need to cry; just be there. Support her need to take on the world; just be there. When she wants to be president, support her with ideas, with encouragement, with money. Support her during labor, support her during final exams, support her in court or in jail or when she applies for assistance. When she says she wants to become a doctor, support her. When she says she wants to end her marriage or start a new one, support her. Just be there beside her. Ask *How can I support you?* Then listen carefully to the answer. Support her by making dinner now and then, by faxing her resume, by postponing a date just to give your support.

Surprise

Surprise yourself today. Say something you never dreamed of saying to someone you never dreamed you could speak to. Do something unpredictable. Have tea instead of coffee; eat dinner sitting on the floor; wear lipstick or leave the lipstick off. Let others be surprised. Smile when they ask *What's going on?* Go swimming at lunchtime, take a yoga class after work, make plans to take a bus to Kentucky. Call someone you know will be shocked and delighted to hear your voice. Wear red. Wear black. Don't wear anything. Give the doorman a rose. Give the bus driver some Gummi bears. Put your car up for sale. Better yet, give it away. Surprise!

Surrender

Give in, give over to something larger than yourself. Sink to the floor and cry and wail, and acknowledge you're lost, confused, afraid. Give in, give over to something wiser than yourself. Stop trying to work out solutions in your brain, and let go of your desire to be in control (which, by the way, is a highly over-rated position). Cry out *It's too hard!* if it feels that way. Yell and scream *It's not fair!* if it isn't. When you're through kicking and screaming, just surrender. Stop strategizing, stop running your life through a "what-if" spreadsheet. Just give in. Through your tears, imagine a place where you can drop off a basketful of your pain, fear, and darkness and say *Here, it's yours* to a kindly soul who will return your emotional laundry in a cleaner, crisper form. But first, you must say *I surrender.*

Survive

Get through it. Cry if you must, bleed if you must, eat potatoes day after day if you must, but survive. Survive the disappointments that come at you like machine-gun fire. Survive the fact that they all died and you survived. Survive on a diet of faith, hope, grit, and prayer. Get through it. Somehow, some way. Ask for help so you can survive. Ask for money, ask for food. Beg and plead if you must. Survive whatever they throw your way. Steel yourself, or collapse. Whatever you must do to survive, do it. Survive another hour, another day, another lifetime. Through the threats, survive. Through the pain, survive. For every woman who ever did and every woman who never could, you must, you will, survive.

Swear

Swear you'll never do it again, and then don't. If you swear on a stack of bibles, you'd best not be kidding. To clean out your pipes once in a while, swear up one side and down the other. Use every *#!!@#$*!!ing swear word you know and some you've never even heard of. When you meet someone who feels as strongly as you do about good grammar and proper etiquette, swear an eternal friendship. Swear by the blessed and inconstant moon. Swear to live your whole truth and nothing but your truth. If he won't leave you alone, swear out a warrant for his arrest. When he swears it will never happen again, swear you've heard it all before.

Swoon

Let yourself be taken by a sensation that's so powerful that your legs turn to jelly and you sink to the floor. Bite into a ripe, juicy peach still warm from the summer sun, and swoon with the deliciousness of it all. Swoon when your eyes meet the eyes of your beloved—and you haven't even met yet! Swoon over the absolute perfection of a double rainbow in a backlit twilight sky. Let the awesome power of nature flood your senses and melt your mind. Swoon when you see a regal blue heron glide over the surface of a crystal-clear lake. Swoon when you hear the merry sound of a Celtic harp floating over a high garden wall. When you step through that doorway that brings you into a union of spirit and soul, swoon in divine ecstasy. Be open enough to drink in every luscious morsel that life sends your way. And when you can't stand any more, swoon.

Take

Take your time. Take a deep breath. When you've done an outstanding job, stand up and take a bow. **Take yourself seriously** and others will, too. When things get hot and heavy, take a chill pill. Take others at their word—and take them to task if they don't follow through. **Take charge** when the situation demands it: when you're asked, or when no one else will, or when it's obvious that you're the woman to take the reins. Take the bull by the horns and wrestle him to the ground with your bare hands. **Always take a moment before you speak.** Take a moment to compose yourself. Take another breath. Loosen up and take a chance. Close your eyes and take a leap of faith. Stop taxiing the runway already, and **take off!**

Talk

Talk it out, talk it through, talk it over, talk it
up. Talk about world affairs, talk about politics,
talk about terrorism, talk about the state of the
economy. Oh, yeah—talk about men, talk about
other women, talk about shoes, talk about soap,
talk about everybody's kids, talk about your
laundry detergent (well, talk about it from an
environmental standpoint). Talk about life, talk
about death, definitely talk about sex. Talk about
how good it is, how nonexistent it is, how silly it
is, how different it is or might be with men or
with women, and who is or isn't having it anyway. Ask a friend to listen because you just have
to talk. Talk on the phone a lot. Talk to your
kids and hope that some of it sinks in. Talk dirty,
talk a little trash. Talk in bed, talk over food, talk
on an airplane. Remember that *talk is cheap* —
and value what you say accordingly.

End of talk.

Taste

Take a taste before you *yonk* the whole thing. Get a taste of the job before committing yourself. Taste the flavor of freedom before you swallow it whole. Dip your toe before you dive in all the way. Taste sushi before you swear you don't like it. Taste a burger after all these years. If something leaves a bad taste in your mouth, spit it out. That goes for ideas, opinions, experiences as well as food. Get a taste of city living before you sell the farm. Ditto for country life before you sell the townhouse. Try accordion music; you might find out you like it! Taste the twenty-seven-mile commute before you accept the promotion. Accept that some things you can't taste beforehand, like childbirth, death, or the presidency of the United States. Always exercise good taste—but, of course, that goes without saying.

Teach

Teach a young girl something that an old woman once taught you. If it never happened, teach what you wish you had learned. First, teach yourself. Teach patience. Teach tolerance. Teach a song that your people sang hundreds of years ago. Teach a story that was handed down from great-grandmother to grandmother to mother to daughter. Teach a circle dance. Offer to teach that one special thing you do. Teach yourself something that no one ever taught you—like changing the oil in your car or making yogurt from scratch or putting up a fence—and then pass it on. Whatever you learn, teach it to another woman. Teach others how to be a well woman by being one yourself.

Tell

Tell the truth. For the first time, tell three people that you love them. Tell two others that their words or their actions hurt you. Tell how much it hurt. Tell a friend something you never told anyone before. Make up a story about a strong, brave princess and a flying horse, and tell it to your favorite young girl. It's not too late to go ahead and tell him you're sorry. After all these years, tell her you forgive her. Or don't. Tell the truth. Tell the story that no one else can tell. Tell a lover how good it feels when your lips meet. Tell something good. Smile when you say it. Tell the boss, with all due respect, that she was out of line. Tell a joke. If people laugh, tell another. Tell that annoying man to get lost. Tell him again. Tell yourself you're beautiful, tell yourself you deserve the best of everything. Tell it to your inner child, tell it to your inner parent, but don't tell anyone, real or imagined, who will judge you or cause you to disbelieve anything you choose to tell yourself.

Thank

Always be grateful. Give thanks for all that you have, no matter how little or how much that may be. Thank your grandmother for wonderful cheekbones, thank your fourth-grade teacher for getting you that special book on how bridges are built. When you get through another day, say *Thank you* to God or Goddess or whoever you believe is in charge. Be thankful for the music that leaves make when tickled by a warm breeze; be thankful for rain. When your promotion comes through, say *Thank you*. When a friend lets you sleep on her sofa because you can't be anywhere else, say *Thank you*. Be thankful that you have two arms and legs that work. If you don't, be thankful you still have a heart with which to give thanks.

Think

Use your head. After you intuit, reflect, and discern, think. Think about the consequences of your actions. Think about their impact on the next seven generations. Think about right and wrong; think about what matters most. What *really* matters. Before you jump to offer assistance, take a moment and think. Do you have the time? The energy? The desire? Think about your reasons for offering. Are your motivations pure, your intentions clear? Take just a moment to think. Take a weekend, if that's what you need. Balance your heart with your head. Ask them to wait while you think things through. If you need more time, ask them again. Before you speak, think about what you're going to say, and what others are likely to hear. If you start to obsess about what others will think, stop! You've been thinking too long.

Thrive

Once you get past *survive*, move on up to *thrive*. Figure out what it takes for you to be radiant—and see that you get as much as you need. Thrive on attention (most of us do!); thrive on challenge. If you don't thrive in the city, move to the gulf; if you don't thrive there, move to the desert or the mountains or the equator. Thrive on physical activity; thrive on peace and quiet. Fill yourself up with the perfect customized blend of nourishment, and become your most brilliant and beautiful self. Glow with good health, exude good cheer, and watch good fortune rain upon you. Thrive on the joy of being alive. Thrive on home cooking, on the love of a growing circle of friends. Surround yourself with thriving, vibrant women, and soak up the energy that will help you to thrive.

Throw

Throw yourself into something new. Throw on an old pair of jeans and throw on a big, baggy sweater and throw around a football. Throw an awesome pitch at the Saturday morning softball game. Throw another log on the fire. Throw pieces of popcorn into the air and catch them with your tongue. Throw raisins, throw M&M's. Don't throw yourself into a tizzy over nothing! If they absolutely refuse to listen, throw your weight around. Throw up your hands and walk away. Throw in the towel. Learn to throw on a potter's wheel. (Yeah, throw those first attempts into the back of the closet.) Throw caution to the wind. When someone throws you a bone, throw it right back with a snarl.

Tie

Tie brightly colored helium balloons to your mailbox so people will know where you live. Tie an entire handful of yarn around a hatband and tie beads and buttons on the ends. Tie the knot (but not so tightly that it ties you down). Tie up all your loose ends before you move on. Strengthen your family ties or cut them altogether. Tie twine around a cardboard box and call it a suitcase. Tie rope around a tree branch and call it a swing. Yes, yes, tie up the telephone for hours. *Please tie your shoelaces so you won't trip!* Go for the win and be happy to tie. Tie the all-time sales record. When the chemo takes your hair, wrap silky scarves around your head and ask a friend to tie them in strong, lovely knots that won't slip.

Touch

Press up ever so lightly, and touch.
Touch fingers, touch toes, be knocked
off your feet by the touch of those two
perfect lips. Touch gentle, touch firm.
Graze the back of another's hand with
your own. Touch the part of your own
body that you love. (*Come on, there's got
to be at least one!*) Touch the trunk of a
tree with your cheek, close your eyes,
and slowly turn your face and let the
sun and the wind and the rain touch
your soul. Touch others with kindness,
with your own pure heart. Touch
another without ever touching skin to
skin. Take away the *ouch* in *touch*.
Practice the sacred art of touch, and
discover how touching life can be when
you allow yourself to touch and be
touched.

Trade

Support free trade. Trade your hair rollers for roller skates; trade your laptop for a lapdog. Trade clothes, trade stories, gather up all the earrings you never wear and trade them for one fabulous pair that you always will. Trade a foot rub for a manicure. Trade two Superbowl tickets for a one-way ticket to Paris. Make sure it's first class. Trade a morning of child care for an evening of cat care. For just one day, trade your car for a bicycle. Trade your excess zucchini for her extra tomatoes. Trade your boring Tuesday evenings for a tap dancing class. Trade insults with that totally rude woman down the road. Trade a panful of your sister's homemade tiramisu for a bowl full of Jell-O with marshmallows. Hmmmm. On second thought, don't.

Transform

Change everything you touch. Transform yourself, and see how everyone around you is suddenly transformed. Transform your fear into strength, your confusion into clarity, your judgment into love. Transform your relationships with your parents, with your children, with the universe. Transform your thoughts into action, your ideas into reality. Transform that dark and dingy back room into a light and airy writing space. Transform your bedroom into a serene and sacred temple. Now transform yourself into the goddess who lives there. Transform that old, beaten-up green trunk into a place where magic dwells. Transform two carrots, some leftover noodles, half an onion, and a few drops of olive oil into a dinner for three. Transform these simple words into a prayer for transformation.

Travel

Get out of town! Travel to the next county, the next state, the next continent. Experience something different for a change. View a different landscape, a bigger skyscape. Meet people who talk differently from you, who look different, who *are* different. Be a tourist. Go to a church social where you don't know a soul. Attend a lecture on a topic you barely knew existed. Prowl around a strange library. Eat a breakfast the likes of which you've never tasted. Lift yourself out of your everyday routine, and enter a room filled with new sounds, sights, tastes, and textures. If you find you never want to go back, don't travel that road again.

Treasure

Recognize the value of what really matters to you, and treasure it. Treasure your time and take care not to kill it. Treasure the friend who never judges you and who carries you in her heart always, no matter what you do. Treasure every moment, and know that they can never be replicated. Treasure each and every day as a blessing. Treasure the sunshine—and when you are blinded by its heat and light, treasure the ever-so-faint breeze that wafts against your cheek. Look closely at the columbine in full summer splendor, and see it for the jewel it is. Treasure your health, and do whatever you can to polish it up to a dazzling glow. Treasure your pastor, your priestess, your rabbi, your spiritual counselor—anyone who gently helps you find your way.

Take nothing for granted.

Treasure everything.

Tremble

Give yourself the freedom to tremble without fear. Tremble when there's so much electricity in the room that it has nowhere to go but right through you. Tremble when you hear a woman open her mouth and sing a song so pure and so divine that it must have come from the angels themselves. Tremble at your own power. Tremble when you're surrounded by thousands of women holding candles under a moonless sky, walking arm in arm and taking back the night for women everywhere. Sit on top of a mountain at twilight; sit with other believers in a church or a synagogue or tipi or temple or on a basement floor or on a forest floor—and tremble at all the things you can never explain.

Triumph

Beat the odds. Triumph over every bit of adversity ever flung into your path, every hardball ever thrown squarely into your face. Triumph over the system that wanted to keep you down—even while claiming it wanted to lift you up. Triumph over bad fortune, bad luck, bad karma. Emerge triumphant when everyone said you could never do it, when everyone said it could never be done, when everyone said you should never even try. Triumph in the face of thousands of years of oppression. Dig a little deeper, push a little harder. Triumph over all of it. Triumph over small, ignorant minds. Triumph over the danger and the pain. Struggle and bleed and crawl that last mile on your hands and knees, but triumph. When all is said and done, triumph!

Trust

Stop second-guessing yourself. You know what you know, you know? That inner tickling is your highest truth. It will serve you well; the backfire comes when you deny or discount it. Take in information from all sides and yet trust, in the end, that you—and you alone—know what's best for you. If all day you pine to paint, then that is what you must do. If you ache to walk beside the ocean, find a way to get there. Trust your own instincts against the education of any doctor, any lawyer, anyone who spouts facts and platitudes and absolutes. Learn to listen to your gut. Without complete trust, you are left only to rust.

Try

Pick up a flute and try to play it. Think of sweet words, then try to say them. Want to be stronger, softer, kinder, firmer, funnier, wiser? Try. Especially, try things that scare you half to death. Try to fix the lamp (first unplug it). Try to show a bit more compassion for the arrogant woman at work. The one with the horrible hair. Just try. Try eating your bagel without any cream cheese at all, not even veggie lite. Just this once. Try reflecting instead of analyzing; try intuition instead of logic. Just try for the heck of it. Try loving another woman as much as you love a man. Or vice versa. Just try. Try skydiving, try stand-up comedy, try politics. Don't think about succeeding or failing, winning or losing. Just try.

Try it once, then try again.

Twirl

Stretch out your arms, throw back your head, and twirl until you fall to the ground in dizzy ecstasy. Own at least one twirling skirt that spirals up while you spiral around. Better yet, a crinoline slip. Twirl on the dance floor, on the kitchen floor, on that flat part of grass in the neighborhood park. Look up while you twirl, close your eyes while you twirl. Twirl in an elevator or while waiting in line for your driver's license. Find three other women to twirl with on the sidewalk. Be a whirling, twirling foursome. Go in different directions. Be sure to look quizzically at other people who are walking back and forth in straight lines while all the while you twirl.

Understand

Always try to understand that you can't always understand.

Try to understand what it's like to be dirt poor, to be thirteen and pregnant and scared and alone and strung out on crack. Try to understand the meaning of existence. Try to understand how some parents can toss their baby girls into the garbage or sell them for a month's wages. Try to understand the health care system in the United States. Go ahead, try. Try to understand why some women don't try harder, or why they can't. When a woman explains why she has stayed in an abusive relationship, try your best to understand. Try to understand why some women love women, why some women love men, why some women can't love at all. When you understand that you may not always be able to understand, then—*Aha!*—you're beginning to understand.

Undulate

Oh, yeah! Unhinge that pelvis and move!
You can do it. Exotic dancers do it, African
dancers do it, pregnant women do it.
Women who have met and embraced that-
which-lies-below-the-waist do it best of all.
You can do it. Say *Good day* to your belly,
and smile. Plant your feet on the ground or
on the carpet or on the kitchen floor. Let
your consciousness slide down from your
head like an elevator—and land in your
belly. Forward and back, side to side, tilt
and swirl. (Cover up the mirror. This is
about feeling, not looking.) Steal a few
moments in the women's bathroom at work,
and practice. At the mall, when you think
no one's paying attention, undulate. It's
good for digestion, good for sex, good for
your soul. *Undu* your pelvis before it's too
late. Undulate!

Unleash

Let 'er rip!

Unleash your passion and woe be unto those who aren't ready for you! Unleash your vast and limitless creative powers—and watch what you bring forth from your hands, from clay and paper, wood and wheat. Unleash your ability to heal, and let the healing begin. Unleash your physical strength and start running up hills and swimming across channels and trekking in your wheelchair. Unleash your mind! Break free from old, boxy, limited ways of thinking, and radiate your genius throughout the lecture hall and the laboratory and the lunchroom. Stop holding back your compassion, your insight, your laughter, your innate wisdom, your boundless capacity for living. Warn them if you will, for when you cut the reins and the leash comes off, the power most definitely goes on.

Unravel

Unravel the story that is your life. Untangle the knots, and take a long look at what has held it all together. Where is it twisted, where is it the most beautiful? What loose ends still hang—and how might they best be tied off? What connections have become frayed, what small chinks have grown into daunting chasms? Commit to unravelling the greater mysteries: the whys and wherefores that hold sway over your existence. Draw back the curtains and let new light shine in. Disengage from the jumble of events and emotions, and pick up the thread you dropped along the way. Examine the complexity of your own self, the sheer intricacy of the journey that is your life: what a marvel to unravel!

Untie

Loosen up! Untie your shoes and run barefoot through the grass —you're likely to untie some of the knots in your stomach and neck, too. Slip into something more comfortable, like a less restrictive job or a relationship based on freedom instead of fear. Forget the apron strings—those that attach you or attach others to you. The finding is in the unbinding. Untether yourself from the chains that keep you from exploring every nook and cranny of your world. Tug ever so gently at the strings that you believe are holding everything together. How do they truly keep you apart—and from what? Isn't it time you try to untie?

Use

Use that which you have been given. If you have two good legs, get out of the car and use them! If you have a brain, use it. If you have any eyesight left at all, read to someone who doesn't. If you believe that you have a gift for healing, use it— -no matter what others say. Use your smile, your humor, your ability to bring people together. Use it, use it, use it. Use your sweet voice, your tender heart, your ability to fix anything. Use it, use it, use it. Use your money wisely and generously. Use your gifts the same way. If you can coax melodies out of a flute, share the music. If you can sell like no one else, raise money for your favorite cause. Whatever you have, use! If you don't, we all lose.

Venture

Venture out into uncharted waters. Venture
forth with courage and with a glorious
sense of adventure. When someone asks
you a question and you don't know the
answer, venture a guess. Venture being
wrong. Venture being ridiculously wrong.
Venture deep into your own being. Into the
deepest recesses of your soul. Risk finding
the unexpected. Risk not liking what you
find. Venture into your inner landscape,
into the places that have become barren
and inaccessible and foreboding. Venture
the possibility that they could become
green and growing again, nourished and
rich and alive. Venture into a time of winter, and know with certainty that spring
will spring again.

Visit

While you're in the neighborhood, visit. While the wash is still washing, visit. Visit over the back fence, if you have one. Visit in the grocery store, in the canned soup aisle. Invite yourself up for a visit. Visit an old friend from elementary school. Visit your mother's last remaining friend. Visit anyone in the hospital who asks you to visit. Invite the girls down the block for a visit. Invite their dolls, too. Visit light; visit simple. Stop long enough to have a soda or coffee or an ice cream, and visit. Don't hold a meeting; just visit. Don't throw a party; just visit. Bring out a plate of crackers and an apple cut into wedges, and be with each other and visit.

Wait

When you feel most pressured to answer or act, wait. Wait a moment or two before speaking. Wait three days before deciding. Wait until all your inner turmoil settles and your answer rises to the top with crystal clarity. Make them wait, even if it makes them a bit crazy. When you've planted new seeds in your life, you must simply wait until it's time for them to bloom. Things happen when they happen, and your wishing, willing, pleading, and jumping up and down won't speed up the process. Wise women know to wait and how to wait. Wait patiently. Wait with dignity. If you've been taught to hate waiting, turning your attention somewhere else may help the time go faster. Better yet, learn to wait doing nothing at all.

Walk

Walk in the morning to start your day on the right foot. Walk to solve any problem, answer any question. Walk barefoot whenever you can. Walk on the grass instead of the sidewalk; walk on the sand instead of the grass. Walk tall, even if you're four-foot-eleven. When he won't listen, walk away. When she disses people or things that matter to you most, walk out. Walk to the store, walk to the movies, walk to work. Point yourself in the right direction, and just walk. Walk your path in beauty, walk in joy. At night, walk with eyes on the soles of your feet. Walk around the block and collect your thoughts. Walk around the neighborhood and collect litter. Walk into the center of the circle, the spiral, the labyrinth, and walk back out again. Walk, don't run. Walk where you usually drive, and notice all you never noticed. If you're talking without walking, then it's just so much talk.

Wane

Withdraw with the moon. Go
inward. Move away from the
hustle and bustle of productivity
and outward activity. Honor
your urge to pull back, to quiet
yourself. Heighten your sensitiv-
ity to your surroundings, to the
way they affect your energy and
your attitude. Stay a bit closer to
home, stay warm, stay rested.
Stay open to dreams, visions, and
ideas that may come to you when you wane.

Respect your cycles, your
energetic ebb and flow.
Choose this time to be
alone, to close the drapes
and turn down the phone.
Let yourself wane, and
trust in the knowledge
that you'll soon wax again.

Wax

Wax with the moon,

growing toward fullness and abundance. Feel the pull to expand, to create, to move out of the darkness and make real your vision in the world. Come out of your quiet egg place. Show a bit more of your face. Dance, or paint, or sculpt your dream. Build and expand and grow your business. Get on the phone and propose your project. Now, while the energy is waxing, let your productivity soar. Reserve a performance space, talk to a publisher, knit a sweater, enclose the new addition, join a campaign. Be more full and available now, more outgoing and more social, more bright and vibrant and waxing all the while.

Transcend

Rise above it. Transcend your limits and exceed all expectations. Raise yourself above the pettiness and the negativity that so often rule the day. Spend time in the woods if it helps you transcend. Meditate if it helps you transcend. Transcend your old, tired needs. Transcend your need to be the best, to be the center of attention, to be the one who holds it all together. Transcend all those years of being told you were ugly, you were hateful, you deserved nothing but crumbs. Transcend the details of when you were born, where you were born, and whom you were born to. Rise above it all to become fully who you were born to be. Live in a universe without end. Transcend.

Weave

Weave your life into a rich tapestry of color and form. Weave a golden cloth and hang it on your front door. Weave a fine tale to share when the moon is full. With the steady, back-and-forth rhythm of the loom to guide you, weave your dreams into reality. Over, under, over, under. Pull together this loose end and that loose end. Tuck in the end that's threatening to fray. Weave your home life into your work life into your inner life, blending them into a strong and lovely whole. Vary the strands. Weave together all that is strong and coarse, tender and delicate, straight and crinkled. Weave the expected and the unexpected, the perfect and imperfect, into a whole cloth that is yours alone.

Weep

When you can't contain another drop, let your heart flow. Weep when the joy is so profound you can do nothing else. Weep when the pain is so searing and so deep you need to wash out every crevice in your body and soul. Weep in the movie theater—even though your tears have nothing to do with what's playing. Weep from utter exhaustion. Let your tears sneak out of your eyes and roll slowly down your cheeks until you can lick them with your tongue. Sob and wail and weep until your shoulders heave and your eyes are red, and every tear has been wrung out of you like a once-dripping washcloth. Weep for every good reason you know and for no reason at all. Weep even when you think it's the wrong place, the wrong time, with the wrong people. And after you weep, sleep.

Whine

Whine whine whine whine whine whine whine.

All right, that's enough.

Feel better?

Whisper

Discover how powerful a whisper can be. When everyone else is shouting, whisper. When the baby is crying, whisper. Whisper into a nearby ear. Say *I think you're wonderful* or *You have chocolate smeared across your shirt*. At the front of the room, at the lectern, with a microphone in your hands, whisper. Whisper in the dark, in the woods. Bend down and whisper to something much smaller than you. Practice bringing your whisper down into nothingness, until you can whisper silently. Once you learn to whisper, you may never need to shout again.

Whistle

Whistle while you work. Whistle while you play. Whistle a happy tune so no one will suspect you're afraid. Whistle the theme from "The Andy Griffith Show," and you'll never, ever, *ever* get it out of your head. Whistle with a mouthful of crackers and peanut butter. Try, just try, to whistle and laugh at the same time. When a performance sends tingles up your spine and energy through your body, clap and cheer and whistle and stomp. Learn to whistle with two fingers in your mouth. With all your fingers in your mouth. Put a perfect blade of grass between your thumbs, and whistle. You're never too old to learn to whistle. Now, while nobody's looking, try it. Whistle.

Wiggle

Wiggle your way out of anything. When they tell you there are no more openings, wiggle your way in anyway. Wiggle your way past Security. Wiggle your way into the VIP section. Wiggle that switch until it switches. Wiggle that knob until it clicks into place. Wiggle on your belly like a snake to reach that wiggly plank in the fence. When your son asks you to wiggle his loose front tooth, ask if you can wiggle out of the request. Wiggle the old screen door until it finally opens. If you can wiggle out of the chairmanship, do it. If you can wiggle your way onto the advisory board, do it. To make sure you're alive, wiggle your fingers and toes. To converse with a bunny, wiggle your nose.

Wild

Free up the wolf, tiger, snake, bear, or lioness
that lives inside you, and let go of the reins!
Howl at the moon, whoop at the stars. Stop
playing nice girl, good girl, make-everybody-
happy girl. Show your fangs now and then. Bare
your claws. Free yourself by dancing to the beat
of an African drum. Once in a while, drop to
the floor and slither, or claw a tree trunk and
growl. Unleash yourself in the privacy of your
own bedroom or your own bathtub, until you're
ready to unloose your wild side in polite society.
If your untamed self has been in hibernation a
long, long time, coax it out with the help of
wild women. Like that redhead down the block
who moves with the grace of a leopard. Like the
woman who sells wildcrafted herbs at the farm-
ers' market. Like Tina Turner. Watch for signs
of the wild in other women. Learn to pick up
the scent and join in and be wild.

Wonder

Let yourself wander with wonder. What if the sky were gold? Draw it. What if your house were a tent? Live it. What do angels sound like? Sing it. Stare for hours at a wild hive of bees. Think about the queen, surrounded by thousands of drones attending to her every whim. Let your mouth fall open at the wonder of it all. Wonder about yourself. What if I did this differently? What if I chose different friends? What if I allowed myself to be totally me? Write a new script. In Act Two, change costume. Make a flashier entrance. A more defiant exit. What would happen if you allowed a bit of wonderment in everything you do?

I wonder.

Work

Work for money or work for love, but work. In your home, on a farm, in a factory, in an office on the forty-third floor. Work to keep a roof over your head and food on the table; work to keep your family together. Work in a uniform, in a suit, in jeans, in overalls, in an apron. Teach, design, serve, build, harvest, sell, manage, drive. Work with your hands, with your heart, with your mind, with your back. Work for something that matters. Work so that others may live in peace, so that children may be born healthy to healthy mothers, so that our cities are safer and our laws are more just. Work at a job you can be proud of. If your work leaves you drained and unhappy, frustrated and resentful, admit that it isn't working out—and work your way into something new.

Wrap

Wrap your arms around your own shoulders when you're feeling lonely. Wrap your arms around your knees and rock back and forth when your spine is feeling tight. After bathtime, wrap someone you love in a big, dry towel to ward off the chill. Wrap a baby in a soft flannel blanket and tuck in the ends so she feels safe and secure. Wrap yourself in a blanket, too. Wrap the tiniest things in bits of colored tissue paper and tie them with yarn and hide them until someday, unexpectedly, someone finds them. Wrap up the discussion before it gets too long, wrap up the meeting early, then go home and wrap your legs around the legs of your favorite, um, er . . . chair. When you're wrapped too tightly, unwrap.

Write

Pick up something and write. Use a fountain pen with ink from a bottle. Write a few words on the back of a postcard. *Wish you were here. Miss you. Love you. Thanks.* Write notes telling people what it means to have them in your life. Write a lot or a little. Write a poem that rhymes and one that doesn't. Write scathing, seething diatribes and never send them. Write a one-act play. Write your grocery list in a beautiful script. Write a note and leave it in a public place where who knows who will find it. Write to a woman you haven't talked to in twenty years. Don't apologize, just write. Write from the core. Don't worry about grammar, don't worry about form. Write how it felt when you got the news, how your feet were melting into the floor, how you turned into a butterfly clinging to the underside of a branch in a hailstorm. Let the words tumble out, upside down, spilling across a scrap of paper you pulled out of the recycling box. Get up like a woman and write.

Yearn

Want it bad! Want it so much it hurts. See it everywhere you look, in your dreams and awake. Taste it, smell it, feel it glide over your skin. Yearn for the touch of your beloved's hand. Yearn for a beloved. Yearn to be touched. Yearn to be free as a cloud. Yearn for a cool breeze on a stultifying summer day. Yearn for more sun on the shortest day of the year. Feel the yearning in the pit of your belly. Feel it in your toes. Feel your heart want to leap out of your body with yearning. Yearn to be alone, to be together. Yearn to leap into the sky and never land. Yearn for that one precious moment. Yearn to be so entirely who you are that you'll hardly recognize yourself.

Yes!

Yes! the invitation to spend a weekend on the Sound. Yes! the offer to set up the new office in Italy. Yes! the request to head up the union effort. Yes! the proposal to buy out the boss and run the store all on your own. Yes! the new hairdo that opens up your face and shows off your eyes. Yes! the opportunity to go back to school. Yes! the road trip to Louisiana. Yes! the three-week backpacking trip. Yes! the petition demanding safer streets. Yes! the invitation to tell your story to troubled adolescent girls. Yes! the apology that took seventeen months. Yes! the fear and trepidation. Yes! the joy, and Yes! the love,

and Yes!

and Yes!

and Yes!

the life.

About the Author

Rachel Snyder is a woman divinely inspired and fully committed to being all the human being she can be. Whether parenting her son and daughter, writing anything and everything from books to news releases to scripts for an overseas home shopping channel, performing stand-up comedy, selling shoelaces in the local shopping mall, appearing in women's community theater, or sipping chai tea at her favorite coffeehouse, she brings extraordinary determination, faith, and inspiration to women and men seeking greater freedom, wholeness, and spirit to their lives. Rachel Snyder was born, grew up, went to college, got a degree, worked at lots of jobs that did their best to block her innate creativity, got married, got divorced 15 years later, made some money and bought some stuff, and later lost it all. But, really, what does it matter? She lives in Boulder, Colorado, for which she is deeply grateful to God.